T0074837

Puppetry, Puppet Animation and the Digital Age

The **Focus Animation Series aims** to provide unique, accessible content that may not otherwise be published. We allow researchers, academics, and professionals the ability to quickly publish high-impact, current literature in the field of animation for a global audience. This series is a fine complement to the existing, robust animation titles available through CRC Press/Focal Press.

Series Editor Giannalberto Bendazzi, currently an independent scholar, is a former Visiting Professor of History of Animation at the Nanyang Technological University in Singapore and a former professor at the Università degli Studi di Milano. We welcome any submissions to help grow the wonderful content we are striving to provide to the animation community: **giannalbertobendazzi@gmail.com**.

Published:
Giannalberto Bendazzi; *Twice the First: Quirino Cristiani and the Animated Feature Film*
Maria Roberta Novielli; *Floating Worlds: A Short History of Japanese Animation*
Bottini, Cinzia; *Redesigning Animation: United Productions of America*

Forthcoming:
Pamela Taylor Turner; *Infinite Animation: The Life and Work of Adam Beckett*
Lina X. Aguirre; *Experimental Animation in Contemporary Latin America*
Marco Bellano; *Václav Trojan: Music Composition in Czech Animated Films*

Puppetry, Puppet Animation and the Digital Age

Rolf Giesen

Edited by
Giannalberto Bendazzi

CRC Press
Taylor & Francis Group
Boca Raton London New York

CRC Press is an imprint of the
Taylor & Francis Group, an **informa** business

A FOCAL PRESS BOOK

CRC Press
Taylor & Francis Group
6000 Broken Sound Parkway NW, Suite 300
Boca Raton, FL 33487-2742

Printed on acid-free paper

International Standard Book Number-13: 978-0-8153-8204-1 (Hardback)

Library of Congress Cataloging-in-Publication Data

Names: Giesen, Rolf, author.
Title: Puppetry, puppet animation and the digital age / Rolf Giesen.
Description: First edition. | Boca Raton, FL : CRC Press/Taylor & Francis
Group, 2019. | Includes bibliographical references.
Identifiers: LCCN 2018031269 | ISBN 9780815382041 (hardback :
acid-free paper)
Subjects: LCSH: Stop-motion animation films--History. | Puppet
films--History. | Animation (Cinematography)--History.
Classification: LCC TR897.6 .G54 2019 | DDC 777/.7--dc23
LC record available at https://lccn.loc.gov/2018031269

Visit the Taylor & Francis Web site at
http://www.taylorandfrancis.com

and the CRC Press Web site at
http://www.crcpress.com

Contents

Series Editor

Giannalberto Bendazzi, currently an independent scholar, is a former visiting professor of history of animation at the Nanyang Technological University in Singapore and a former professor at the Università degli Studi di Milano. We welcome any submissions to help grow the wonderful content we are striving to provide to the animation community: giannalbertobendazzi@gmail.com.

Author

Rolf Giesen is focusing on all facets of animation as a screenwriter, curator, film historian, and lecturer working in Germany and for a few years in China. For two decades, he did exhibitions devoted to the work of stop-motion legend Ray Harryhausen.

Published:
Acting and Character Animation: The Art of Animated Films, Acting and Visualizing. (co-written with Anna Khan)

Introduction: It's Not Just Nostalgia

T HERE ARE TWO PREJUDICES I encounter quite often.

It's animation. It's nice—but it's not a real movie.

I tell them that it's not only a real movie: it's even *more* than a real movie.

There would be no movies without the principle of animation, and this principle will prevail even in a time when there are no cinemas anymore.

And the second prejudice I am confronted with:

3D computers have virtually finished the era of puppets, 2D, cutout, or whatever animation.

There are people who say this in a nicer way. They say that 3D computer animation is the logical consequence of stop-motion animation, with the best qualities of 2D animation on top, and that therefore stop motion is backward and only provides a convenient niche for a small group of eccentrics.

I even meet animators who tell you that they like to take shelter in such a niche, because they cannot imagine that they would ever succeed in what they call the *mainstream*.

A niche is like a cocoon. The whole society is atomizing into a plethora of cocoons. Everything is divided up, while a few global majors take the helm.

As we have become part of a digital "revolution," 3D computer animation has been declared the global standard. This thought is totalitarian. All of a sudden, the tools are going to instruct the artist about aesthetics and which road to take in art.

Yet animation is no one-way road. It's about *variety*, not about what commercialists think should be the singular, beatific tool that is best suited to grind out large quantities of images. In China, for instance, the introduction of digital animation has made it possible to produce more than 260,000 minutes worth of animation annually. But you bet: most of it looks the same. And despite all the tools, if it weren't for market leaders like Pixar or DreamWorks Animation, most 3D animation would look cheap and limited.

That sounds a little bit *heretic*—and it should.

Please let me run my train of thought and try to explain. I could be an advocate of 2D animation as well, which I still consider high art, because it's about drawings and paintings set in motion. But with this book, I decided to stand up for stop motion and puppet animation.

This is, if you prefer, a plea for variety in animation and also for variety in *commercial* animation. This is no plea against digital animation and against tools that make all of animation easier. It is, however, a plea against dulling standardization thanks to the power of the new tools. To my mind, these new tools are given no right to diminish any other type of animation. Two-dimensional or puppet animation shouldn't be subordinate to 3D computer animation but *equal*.

While digital animation is raising a globalized claim, puppet animation has always respected the national identity of its country of origin: Russian stop motion is different from Czech or French or German or Dutch.

Yes, we are aware that "conventional" animation won't be fit for the *intermedia age*, but so are most humans.

To us, the main question shouldn't be about the tools of animation—paper, puppets, digits—but only about the *quality* of animation. Of course, from the standpoint of photo-realism, digital technology will always prevail. But this is certainly not the pivotal question concerning the art of animation and art in general.

Naturalist painting has certainly lost a great deal of power. Photography has forced us into photo-realism that even dominates the realm of fantasy and imagination. This is one of the reasons true artists don't compete with photo-realism anymore and have created new expressions of art.

Why poetry? We have millions of bloggers sharing the latest Tweets!

Why frame-by-frame animation? We get it in real time!

Why still have that jerky "antediluvian" animation if we can make it much more fluid?

Jim Danforth, a dear friend and one of the great American stop-motion animators, once remarked that ballet dancers are moving in an odd way, not at all realistically. But we don't go to a ballet to see real, mundane movements, do we? We go to see artful movement. With stop motion it is the same. We shouldn't expect to see real movement in a stop-motion film.

Art has a lot to with stylization. Gregory Jein, a fine American miniaturist, once went to Japan to work on a postapocalyptic sci-fi flick titled *Virus* (1980). He and his colleagues from Hollywood were surprised to see that their Japanese counterparts didn't care for overall naturalism but enjoyed doing things that were *stylized*. Eiji Tsuburaya, the late "father" of Japanese *Kaiju* films, had in one of his films (*Frankenstein Conquers the World*) a miniature horse being devoured by a rubber-suit monster. He could have used a real horse and made a split screen, but said that the "toy" looked nicer. And right he was. To people like him, naturalism wasn't art and sure wasn't fun. Maybe it's not good to link science fiction with art, but I do remember that, while seeing old science fiction movies, there was always a feeling of childlike innocence. We excuse this unwelcome emotion (and the occasional wire we detect on screen) with the explanation that they didn't have computers back then in film production and couldn't solve it any better. The effects-laden sci-fi blockbuster from our days, with cameras circling around crashing skyscrapers and sound effects that injure your eardrums, may have a lot more to offer but certainly no innocence. Sure, it looks more real than reality, but at the same time, it's rubbish content-wise.

The idea to move images is as old as Stone Age art. The idea to move puppets dates back to ancient times, too. It's great to have computers, but why should we sacrifice the tradition of puppetry for it?

I can talk about this topic only as a historian. Luckily, I am no film semanticist.

I have to thank Giannalberto Bendazzi, who invited me to publish this little pamphlet in his new book series, and my wife, Anna Khan. I want to dedicate it to the memory of the late animation expert and stop-motion sponsor Michael Schmetz.

Rolf Giesen
Berlin and Grambin, Summer 2018

CHAPTER 1

The Origin of Puppets and Homunculi

THE PUPPET, BE IT a hand puppet or a marionette, is an extension of our heart, an extension of our soul.

Breathing life into a puppet, you wish it really would open its eyes and live: the Pinocchio effect. In a way, the puppet has you over a barrel. In stop motion, you are communicating with a puppet like a shaman and the puppet seems to communicate with you, at least in your imagination. A shaman acts as a bridge between different worlds, the material and the spiritual world. There are tales of ventriloquist's puppets, demonic dummies, who have minds of their own and absorb the puppeteer. Michael Redgrave's dummy from *Dead of Night* became the prototype for more *devil dolls* to come. There is slight resentment concerning puppets on behalf of many adults, as they confuse *puppets* with *dolls*.

"Aren't you too old to play with dolls?" Ray Harryhausen was once asked, and since that time he never talked about puppet but *model* animation.

Puppets can be cult objects in the material world, including the Voodoo puppets of black magic. Superstitious people believe them

Puppeteer Gerd Josef Pohl and his Nosferatu marionette. (Photographed by Martin van Elten. Courtesy of Gerd J. Pohl.)

to be cursed. Early shadow and puppet theaters have a religious background. Puppets are materialist manifestations from the spiritual world. Three-dimensional computer animation is only spiritual: it doesn't create material manifestations, only ghost images. The animator cannot touch them.

AN ACT OF MAGIC

Creating puppets is an act of magic: like creating homunculi.

The so-called *homunculus* was the alchemic goal of Doctor Faustus, the legendary necromancer and astrologer who—before he became a durable character in literature—was the star of puppet plays in which he sold his soul to the devil, a predecessor of Frankenstein.

One of these alchemists was Theophrastus Bombast von Hohenheim, otherwise known as Paracelsus, a sixteenth-century master of holistic medicine and natural healing, who is said to have been interested in *artificially made human beings*, a concern that in those days came close to blasphemous *black magic*.

In the second century, Hero of Alexandria even wrote manuals on how to fabricate images of god that would move. He would rotate statues and design a miniature puppet theater—not for entertainment's sake, but for religious purposes. To create a god was to perform theurgy: giving life to inanimate objects. The tradition of animated gods carried on in the fascination with puppets.

There is a classic German short story titled "The Sandman" written by E. T. A. Hoffmann in 1816: A man falls in love with a girl—until he realizes that she is not human. The man's name is Nathanael. He abandons Klara, his down-to-earth fiancée, for a beautiful girl he has seen from his room in a neighboring building. This girl, Olimpia, does nothing but sit motionless in her bedroom. She plays piano, however, as Nathanael learns, and dances with perfunctory precision. When Nathanael talks to her, she only responds with a gentle "Ah, ah!" To his horror, Nathanael realizes that Olimpia is a life-size mechanical doll fabricated by Spallanzani, his physics professor. Olimpia's eyes are made of glass. Inside her body is a clockwork mechanism that controls her movements and dancing.

Olimpia is a relative of Disneyland's Animatronics, and Spallanzani is the ancestor of Walt Disney. Disney was the proverbial puppet master. (There are even some historians who claim that puppetry predates live actors on stage.)

I didn't know that there was such a thing as the World Puppetry Day. And I didn't know that besides the Muppets, there was such a thing as Christian puppetry, a form of Christian ministry through puppetry.

CHAPTER 2

The Art of Silhouette Plays and Films

ONE SPECIAL ART FORM in puppetry is flat. Shadow puppetry may be as old as the discovery of shadows themselves. Folk tales, fables, and legends are favorite topics on the shadow screen in any culture and time period.

Shadow puppets were first made of paper sculpture and later from the hides of donkeys or oxen. That's why their Chinese name is *pi ying*, which means *shadows of hides*. Shadow puppetry was quite successful during the Tang and Song dynasties. Under the rule of Kangxi, the fourth emperor of the Qing dynasty, this folk art became so popular that there were eight generously paid puppeteers in one prince's mansion. When the Manchu emperors spread their rule to various parts of China, they brought the puppet show with them to make up for the fact that they could not appreciate local entertainment due to language barriers. However, for a few years, the art of puppetry hit hard times in the Middle Kingdom. From 1796 to 1800, the government forbade the public presentation of puppet shows to prevent the spreading of peasant uprising at the time. It was not until 1821 that shadow puppet shows gained vigor again.

In Germany, at the end of the Silk Road, the art of the shadow play moved from stage straight to the moving picture screen.

Lotte Reiniger (1899–1981) created the most wonderful silhouette films like the feature-length *The Adventures of Prince Achmed* (*Die Abenteuer des Prinzen Achmed*), which premiered in Berlin and Paris in 1926. Lotte adored actors and dancers, particularly ballet dancers, and she spent many hours watching them in their performances. At a young age, Lotte had entered the Theater School of Max Reinhardt. Here she developed her paper-cutting skills, producing tiny portrait figures with great accuracy, particularly of the stars, in order to attract their attention.

During Germany's financial crisis, Louis Hagen, a banker, had invested in a large quantity of raw film stock as a shelter from inflation, but the gamble hadn't paid off—and so Lotte was allowed to use it to make the Thousand and One Nights fantasy of *Prince Achmed* in the magnificent tradition of the shadow theater, which in fact is one of the founding stones of intercultural synergy between East and West.

The technique of this type of film is fairly simple. As with cartoon drawings, silhouette films are photographed frame by frame, but instead of using drawings, silhouette marionettes are used. These marionettes are cut out of black cardboard and thin lead, every limb being cut separately and joined with wire hinges. A study of natural movement is very important so that the little figures appear to move just as men and women and animals do. The backgrounds for the characters are cut out with scissors as well, and designed to give a unified style to the whole picture.

Describing the process of animation, Lotte Reiniger explained that, before any acting, there is a lot of technique involved to move the flat silhouette puppets around:

> When you are going to play with your figure seriously, make sure that you are seated comfortably. The shooting

will take up a long time and you will have to keep yourself as alert as possible. Don't wear any bulgy sleeves; they might touch your figure unexpectedly and disturb its position. If possible arrange to place an iron or wooden bar 5 in. above the set along your field of action and let your arms rest on it, so that you touch your figure only with the finger-tips, or with your scissors. [...]

The most cautiously executed movements must be the slow ones, where you have to alter the position only the fraction of an inch. A steady, slow walk is one of the most tricky movements to execute. Here the most frequent mistake at the beginning is to let the body lag behind the legs, so that they seem be running away from under the

Lotte Reiniger and assistants at work on *The Adventures of Prince Achmed*. (Courtesy of Primrose Film Productions Ltd. [Caroline Hagen-Hall and Christel Strobel].)

The Adventures of Prince Achmed was released in 1926. (Courtesy of Primrose Film Productions Ltd. [Caroline Hagen-Hall and Christel Strobel].)

body. If you touch the centre of the body first and move it forward, holding the legs in the initial position, you will notice that they fall into the next position almost by themselves.

Tall, lean figures are more prone to these errors than round, short ones, which roll along easily, whilst the balance of the long ones is more difficult to establish. [...]

If a figure is to turn round it had best to do so in a quick motion. If you want the movement slower you might partly hide it in a convenient piece of the setting.[1]

Lotte's interest in silhouette films matched perfectly with the fascination with shadows that she shared with Expressionist filmmakers like Fritz Lang, Robert Wiene, Friedrich Wilhelm Murnau, and Albin Grau, who had designed both *Nosferatu* and *Warning Shadows (Schatten)*. Yet she pointed out that there is a difference between a shadow and a silhouette:

> From the early days of mankind shadows seemed to men to be something magic. The spirits of the dead were called shadows, and the underworld was named the Kingdom of Shadows and was looked upon with awe and horror. [...]
>
> The essential difference between a shadow and a silhouette is that the latter cannot be distorted.[2]

This is an important statement, because distortion is a key feature of 2D and 3D computer animation as we know from Disney to Pixar.

REFERENCES

1. Lotte Reiniger, *Shadow Theatres and Shadow Films*. London and New York: B. T. Batsford Ltd. and Watson-Guptill, 1970, pp. 105–108. Reprinted with kind permission.
2. Lotte Reiniger, ibid., pp. 11–13.

CHAPTER 3

2D versus 3D in Nazi Germany

S ILHOUETTE FILMS WERE PRODUCTS of art and as such acknowledged by art connoisseurs. Alas, their success at the box office was limited. But what about the dimensional puppet film created in stop-motion animation? Interestingly enough, the puppet film precedes hand-drawn 2D animation in film history.

WALKING MATCHSTICKS

The idea was obvious: to use cinematography for something that was the legitimate successor of Edweard Muybridge's *chronophotogaphy*, shooting frame by frame. Some historians claim that Arthur Melbourne-Cooper (1874–1961) might have been the first to do stop-motion animation, at least in Britain. But to assume that Melbourne-Cooper, who started as an assistant to film pioneer Birt Acres, animated matches as early as 1899 is— maybe—only wishful thinking. Anyway, even if these matches were animated later, it doesn't diminish Cooper's achievements. He was still among the first:

> Cooper can be compared to his contemporary Georges Méliès, as both used camera tricks to create worlds of fantasy.

This assumption seems to be right, but is not. The mistake lies in the definition of the term *camera tricks*. It is right that Méliès, the proprietor of le Théâtre Robert-Houdin in Paris, was a conjuror and illusionist and used camera tricks to sell stage magic to a wider audience. On the other hand, Melbourne-Cooper didn't use camera tricks: no split screen, double exposure, ghost images, or anything else—just simple, plain frame-by-frame photography. That's certainly amazing but no trick, although they began to call it *trickfilm*. Instead, it's tiresome work.

Cooper worked in a homely outfit (like most stop-motion animators do) that he would call Alpha Trading Company, not a large glass studio like Méliès had.

> Cooper comes across more as an enthusiast tinkering away in a small studio with boundless energy. His animations are resolutely small-scale, made using matchsticks or ordinary shop-bought toys, but the tiny spaces are filled with movement. Little people made of matches scuttle about playing sports, getting into more and more of a muddle in the process. Toy animals—scurrying mice, scampering dogs and clumsy elephants—make their way into a model ark two by two. A miniature street corner bustles with dolls, teddies and toy cars, each interacting with each other in different ways. Of Cooper's six surviving films the most memorable is *A Dream of Toyland*, widely referred to as *Dreams of Toyland*. Telling the story of a boy visiting a toy shop and subsequently dreaming of toys coming to life, the film consists of an animated sequence—the actual dream—bookended with live action. The animated portion takes place in a single shot, the only overriding narrative is that the action gets more and more chaotic as the sequence

goes on. In every part of the screen there is a story playing out: toys tussle with each other as they barge across the road, a golliwog tries to restore order but falls from a model bus and picks himself up.[1]

In 1907, American film pioneer James Stuart Blackton animated the toy figures of *Teddy Bears*. Melbourne-Cooper's work, toys and matches included, might date from 1908. One year later, a German cameraman, Guido Seeber, did a short film titled *The Match Artist (Der Streichholzkünstler)*.

LADISLAS STAREVICH

In September 1938, influenced by Disney's huge success, German film journalist Frank Maraun* visited Ladislas Starevich in Paris. The Russian exile was a famous puppet filmmaker, *the* great puppet film pioneer, creator of the feature-length *Story of the Fox (Le roman de Renard)*, who hoped to raise some funds for his next project from German sources. Starevich claimed to have found a formula against Disney:

Although he esteems Disney in his kind and doesn't minimize him he dislikes hand-drawn films. They are not to his taste. Drawings in a film, he says, will remain caricatures: with all amusing characteristics, yet caricatures. They are not living entities that touch the soul. The flatness doesn't allow expression of the soul. The drawing cannot have a soul; for a soul you need a body. The body alone is bearer of the soul, it necessitates three dimensions. In a hand-drawn animated film a man's head can be ripped off and moved back again, and the audience will laugh. To living sculptures you cannot do that: "Od sent de la peine," one will feel pain. Contrary to Disney, the animals are no little machines but living entities, almost human.

* That is, Erwin Goelz (1903–1981).

Who has seen *The Story of the Fox* and who knows Disney will find this differentiation very affecting. Starevich's film, compared to Walt Disney's animal grotesqueness, has the advantage of an unlikely higher level of liveliness and naturalism. In his finer, tender, saturated tone of fairy tale, he is closer to our feeling. Against the saucy, clean step of civilisation of the American, the Pole represents convincingly the old Europe with its culture grown in emotion and so rich in tradition. About Disney one can laugh and marvel, but Starevich one has to love.[2]

There are always biographies that lead artists who are interested in movement to a certain type of animation.

While Melbourne-Cooper, the British pioneer, came from camera technique, Ladislas Starevich came from natural history. Starevich was born to Polish parents in Moscow on August 8, 1882. In 1910, he was appointed director of the Museum of Natural History in Kaunas, Lithuania, and began to make documentaries. One of these was supposed to show a combat of stag beetles, but the nocturnal insects kept shutting down when they were going to start filming and the lights went on. Inspired by the work of French cartoonist and animator Émile Cohl, Starevich decided to joint the insects with wire and stage the fight by stop-motion animation. The process of stuffing dead insects and the art of taxidermy led him to produce animal fables à la Jean de La Fontaine after he moved to France because of the Russian revolution.

The most interesting facet in Starevich's professional career is the fact that stop-motion technique allowed him to stay independent and become sort of an alchemist of animation, a Paracelsus of stop motion. In France, he withdrew to a small outfit in Fontenay-sous-Bois, where he was assisted by his wife France and his daughter Irina. One of his more bizarre short films, *The Devil's Ball* (*Fétiche Mascotte*), made in 1933, was selected by Terry Gilliam as one of the 10 best animated films: a dog puppet goes literally through hell to get an orange to a girl dying of scurvy.

Some time ago, we unearthed a memo that was written by German filmmakers more than 75 years ago. It was meant to interest the Nazi powers-to-be in dimensional animation.

It's a propaganda item, of course, but there are some interesting statements that were neglected by the so-called Ministry of Enlightenment and Propaganda that was going for 2D animation Disney-style—and failed in its megalomaniac attempts to outrun Disney in occupied Europe.

DIMENSIONAL ANIMATION IN SPACE

Jürgen Clausen, a producer who seemed to have known Starevich well, turned the animator's ideas into his own. He approached *Tobis Filmkunst* on May 30, 1941, and offered to produce color puppet films as well as to establish a color film studio. Clausen was an expert in both fields: as business and production manager of Gasparcolor Werbefilm G.m.b.H. and Gasparcolor Naturwahre Farbenfilm G.m.b.H., he had specialized in color film stock, and as he had been involved in processing stop-motion films (Clausen reissued Oskar Fischinger's abstract *Composition in Blue* in a special screening of "Color Advertising Films" on October 30, 1938, in Hamburg's Waterloo Cinema) and particularly George Pal's *Philips* shorts, he seemed to be the right choice.

During the war, Clausen, together with Herbert Pohris, provided a memorandum for Tobis Filmkunst in December 1941. Pohris, the coauthor of the memo, was a Berlin painter and member of National Socialist German Workers' Party (NSDAP) since 1931 (no. 724 929). For a monthly fee of RM 1,000 he was hired as consultant, writer-director, and artist-designer. With their memo, both men wanted to talk Tobis into setting up a puppet film studio (if only to please the animated ambitions of the Minister of Enlightenment and Propaganda and his many children). They claimed: we can do better with animated puppets than Disney with animated drawings. In the end, however, the plan failed, but what was suggested is, beyond all Nazi propaganda gibberish, still food for thought:

Who has seen a puppet trickfilm?

There are not many people in Germany who have seen a good puppet trickfilm. Among those who have not one will not find too many who possess enough imagination to acknowledge this special type of form and creation (by cinematic means) as art, only if they deem it similarly high as a live action feature.

Prejudice renders blind!

How does it come that occasionally also film experts cannot link much with the puppet trickfilm? Could it be that they consider it an unreasonable amount of playing around? Such kind of misunderstanding would be possible. However, prejudice shouldn't be declared a dogma.

[…]

A difference—and a recommendation

Here we want to insert the elemental differences between hand-drawn animation and puppet animation because the common distinguishing mark "two-dimensional"— "three-dimensional" is not sufficient; more likely the comparison *Flächen-Trickfilm* [flat trickfilm] and *Raum-Trickfilm* [dimensional animation in space]. (We would also like to introduce this term to give the puppet animation the advantage by which it wouldn't be ridiculed—perhaps this only happens for the use of the term "puppets" or "dolls"—as a kind of "childish play").

What kind of man am I?

There are two ways to see pictures: the "flat" and the "dimensional" kind.—Instead of "flat" in this case we might better term it: "*plakatig*" [poster-like], and instead of "dimensional": "in depth."—As far as I enjoy *plakatig*, i.e. poster-like (hand drawn) trickfilm, I am considered to be more of an intellectual-witty kind of man without the right sense of humor, also *ober-flächig* [superficial] (this is no rating). As far as I am going to enjoy puppet or dimensional trickfilm, I am a spiritually sensual man and have humor. Everybody who has the ability to watch himself will agree to this.—Hand-drawn animation addresses more the intellect. The ideas or improvisations (the American calls them "gags") have only little to do with humor but more with its brilliant superficiality, the *joke*. Hand-drawn animation most often deals with malicious caricatures and likes to parody (the cheap kind to get a feeling of superiority). It is not childlike but more childish. For this reason, notabene, as long as hand-drawn animation will remain "*plakatig*" or poster-like, it will provide an awkward situation to retell German fairy tale content in this particular style (see *Snow White* by Disney!). It doesn't seem advisable at all to film fairy tales, legends and also novels in this way for each content is tied to a certain expression, to its own form.

Hand-drawn animation has more to do with distortion than with grotesque, it invites more to bemusement than guiding us to bonhomie which is reflected in the smile (actually about oneself, i.e. about the own "*Menschlichkeiten*" [humanness] which step out of the mirror of artwork).

Is this a condemnation of hand-drawn animation?— Yes and No! Yes,—regarding the style of previous animation films, and No—regarding the possibilities that lie dormant in this technique. Primarily the following: to give up the "moving poster" and create moving pictorial ornament (without deep illusionistic backgrounds!). As "moving poster" the hand-drawn animated film is an American matter, as moving pictorial ornament it can be as Germanic as, say, a Gothic church window—and in spite of two-dimensionality so "profound" like this. This way, however, lies still ahead!

Disney makes caricature posters

Americans have transferred the *plakatig* hand-drawn animation to its highest degree. This style comes from feuilletonistic comic drawings. The previous hand-drawn animation is—Disney.—Our own Fischer-Koesen, Kaskeline etc. by far don't reach the last perfection of poster *style [plakatig]* and the American humor—they are no Americans, that's it! [...]

Only in Germany!

The puppet or dimensional trick is located in the European cultural space, and no other country can be its more natural home than Germany. The German is deeply dimensionally-romantic, profoundly imaginative, he is dreamy and contemplative. None other succeeds that well in *humorous* grotesque (see Wilhelm Busch) so definitely that one can count it almost into classic art—classic in a sense of perfection of expression. All of this means a splendid, not to say decisive predestination for the dimensional trickfilm and—an obligation. Space and depth oblige the German-Nordic identity. Therefore important results will be accomplished much faster with the German dimensional trickfilm than hand-drawn animation which is burdened with Disney's virtuoso style.

GEORGE PAL

Jürgen Clausen demanded to proceed from George Pal's Puppetoon technique. George Pal, who later became a good friend of Disney (and even resigned from his dream to produce *20,000 Leagues Under the Sea* in favor of Disney's company), was a Hungarian Jew, born Gyula György [Pál] Marczincsák on February 1, 1908, in Cegléd, then Austria-Hungary. He had worked in four countries: in his native Hungary, Germany, the Netherlands, and the United States, in short and feature films, animation and live action.

> Having graduated from the Technical High School in Budapest, George Pal one day happened to stray into a film laboratory, where he learned the technique of trick filming. Confident of his ability to succeed in this field, he later formed a company of his own and produced advertising films for home and foreign firms. To increase his chances he transferred to Germany and obtained in Berlin a situation as trick film designer, and was eventually engaged by *Ufa* as Chief Animation Designer. In eighteen months he produced here 23 advertising films and also worked during this period for the *Scherl Publishing House* that published his *Habakuk* series.

Eventually, Ufa wanted him to rival the popular stop-motion animation made by Starevich and at Julius Pinschewer's Berlin advertising film studio. In March 1930, Pinschewer Film Aktiengesellschaft released a puppet advertising film for Nestlé's milk chocolate, *Kermess in Hollywood: A Puppet Play* (*Kirmes in Hollywood—Ein Puppenspiel*): puppet duplicates of actors Emil Jannings and Buster Keaton face each other in a boxing match. Buster wins thanks to delicious Nestlé chocolate and receives from Miss Arabella's hands the prize money of $1000. Hedwig and Gerda Otto, mother and daughter, had made this short. They were experts in puppet-making and animating.

On October 15, 1931, joined by Paul Wittke, Jr., a Berlin businessman, Pal founded Trickfilm-Studio G.m.b.H. Pal & Wittke and partly switched from 2D to 3D, which became the

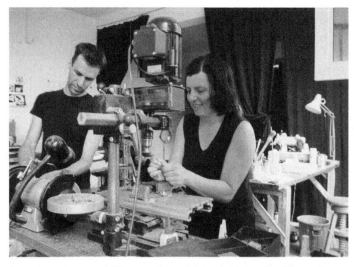

Puppet animators Alberto Couceiro and Alejandra Tomei begin to machine and drill armature parts. (Courtesy of Animas Film.)

The molds for the puppet hands. (Courtesy of Animas Film.)

The finished puppet hands. (Courtesy of Animas Film.)

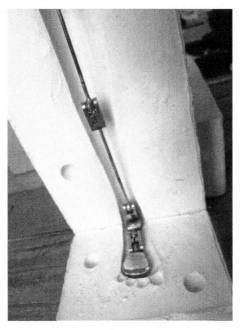

A jointed leg. (Courtesy of Animas Film.)

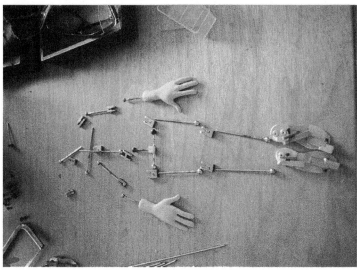

Puppet hands and other parts of the armature are put together.
(Courtesy of Animas Film.)

Alberto Couceiro creates the heads for replacement animation. (Courtesy of Animas Film.)

The finished replacement heads with different mouth movemen (Courtesy of Animas Film.)

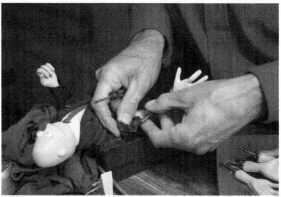

The puppets are dressed and get their hands. (Courtesy of Animas Film.)

basic principle of his later replacement series, produced to great critical acclaim in Eindhoven, Netherlands (for Philips Radio), and Hollywood, CA (for Paramount release).

H. O. Schulze, a Berlin cinematographer, recalled the process of Pal's filmmaking. I interviewed him about his participation in the photographic effects of *Metropolis* (shooting the light rings around the robot), when he suddenly mentioned, en passant, his involvement with Pal and Wittke:

> I became acquainted with George Pal at *Ufa Werbefilm* where I was responsible for model animation photography and for the photographic quality of the cartoons. In 1932, when he decided to leave *Ufa* and establish his own company, Pal asked if I was interested in joining him. He told me that he had something really unusual in mind and that he wanted to equip his new studio in a very up-to-date manner. Always interested in experiments, I accepted. Our first commission was an advertising film for *Oberst Cigarettes*. Pal didn't want to have it drawn frame by frame in the common cartoon fashion but to do it instead with dimensional animation. A blade of tobacco would fold up by itself, glide into a paper husk, stand up, get legs and a head and so on. Then the twenty cigarettes from one package would form a squadron, with an Oberst (colonel) commanding in front, and would march through a futuristic setting which consisted of cigarette packages. The main street of our set was about thirty feet long and ran the whole length of the studio. The cigarettes for each animation step were mounted on boards. All in all, we had approximately sixteen or eighteen boards with squadrons of cigarettes in various walking positions to complete one single walking step which, repeatedly used, resulted in a walking cycle.[3]

In his 1941 memo, Jürgen Clausen enthused about Pal's technique:

We have to proceed from Pal technique!

George Pal is a Hungarian with a specific Balkan enthusiasm for color and love for good-natured grotesque. He comes from hand-drawn animation but has produced dimensional color trickfilms for many years: almost exclusively commercials for Philips, Holland. Although he lost much of his original instinct—in the service of advertisement he has become a little bit Americanized— even his most abstract ideas reflect a somewhat childlike narrator. Therefore, too, his films are so sympathetic to us in spite of their American outfit.

What appeals most to us Germans is the special wood puppet style of Pal's films and the precision of his stop-frame technique. Behind the moving grotesque there is an, albeit originally more technical than artistic, seriousness and diligence. If one observes a Pal animator at the making of technical blueprints, one could think that it would be about the construction of valuable machines.

Color Dimensional Trickfilm will enlighten the whole process of filmmaking—especially color feature films

Pal's films today represent not only an outstanding achievement in the field of color dimensional trickfilm but—and this is essential—in this technique rest possibilities of expression resp. shaping of incredible simplicity and depth. The solution of these tasks will raise the puppet animation film finally into the ranks of artistic high-grade dimensional trick creation, and thus will demonstrate what essentially a *Film-Spiel* [Picture Play] is. (*"Film-Spiel"* should be written as motto above the whole process of filmmaking!)

If one considers that not only an accompanying score (in German tradition) will be added, but also the color of these simple wooden forms (one should think only about

Cézanne's space principle of painted space, of "cone, ball and cylinder") will achieve the most glorious, striking performance so that finally, what hasn't been tried before, one can go to a kind of synchronized element of color and its *dramatic* assessment—not only aesthetical—(which color film development needs so badly) … if one considers all of this, then one will understand why we should proceed from Pal's technique and should acknowledge it as a textbook example sine qua non […].

Then Clausen adds an interesting postscript that proves that he has learned his lesson not only from Pal but from Walt Disney too:

Puppet trickfilm and German toy industry.

In regard to American animation film, a unique insemination of the toy has occurred, which results for instance in the fact that after release of the Mickey Mouse or Pig films and later after *Snow White* and *Pinocchio* not only children's books were published in millions of copies based on the artwork and characters of the Disney production, but also toys, puppets and records invaded European countries (bijouterie: necklaces, buttons, stickers etc.). In Paris, for instance, many shop windows were decorated with characters of the *Snow White* picture. The same is true for the George Pal production in Holland. Here, too, the most prominent characters from various Pal films were absorbed by the toy industry and were exploited.

The German toy industry up until now was leading in the whole world, especially the German children's puppet industry. We are absolutely sure that out of German puppet film production an equally extensive as well as necessary insemination of German toy industry will result, so that later an interaction will occur: puppet trickfilm will support toy industry and vice versa. Add to it that Pal's technique (use of simple work forms like cone, ball, cylinder etc.) is well suited for mass production. This is the technically best prerequisite for animated film featuring plastic color bodies and on the other hand simplifies the transfer into efficient production methods of the toy industry.

The toy industry will have to learn from color dimensional trickfilm if it wants to play the role again, particularly as an export industry in the wide world as it has done before.

Clausen's clear objective was to create feature-length puppet films in color. A puppet feature wouldn't be more expensive than a regular feature, he concluded. Although he cited the self-proclaimed "Führer" of the so-called Third Reich, nobody would listen to him. Instead Clausen was dispatched to the front. On March 14, 1944, a trade paper (*Film-Kurier*) reported Clausen's death as combat cameraman.

The Nazis wouldn't support his idea of dimensional trickfilms, but tried to compete with Disney himself by establishing a 2D factory, even nurturing the absurd idea of building a huge cartoon plant on occupied Crimea Island. Yes, they even used former Pal employees who were originally signed by Clausen—not for dimensional but—paradoxically—for 2D animation.*

THE DIEHL BROTHERS

When they produced puppet films, like the Diehl Brothers in their studio in Gräfelfing near Munich, Germans were not grinding out lively Puppetoons but mainly cozy Biedermeier kitsch, slow-moving like a snail, not shown in cinemas but in schools and at the front. The Diehls definitely occupied a niche, no more, with no chance of going mainstream.

---

* According to the late animation artist Gerhard Fieber.

The Diehl Brothers' idiosyncratic creation of art:
Film Studio for ... Puppets
A well-organized fairy tale world little known to the audience

Under this headline, one of the German trade magazines covered Diehl's production in 1941:

> br. Munich, 17 January. Our fourth visit with Munich filmmakers this time takes us outside of the city gates, to Gräfelfing. There everybody knows the house and the small studio of the Diehls, the birth place of many fairy tale puppet films which thanks to their superior artistic quality stay in the leads. Alas, with the exception of the fairy tale picture *The 7 Ravens (Die sieben Raben)* almost none of their work has reached the general audience, because these Munich filmmakers for years work exclusively for *Reichsanstalt für Film und Bild in Unterricht und Wissenschaft*, the Reich Institute for Film and Image in Education and Science. [...]
>
> Maybe it is no coincidence that, particularly, Munich artists are leading in puppet films if one considers that Munich can look back onto many decades of traditional work in the field of puppet theater. In Munich Count Pocci [who wrote more than 40 marionette plays] and Father [Josef Leonhard] Schmid worked as promoters and revivers of the puppet play. The Diehls have adopted this art form and have translated it to the cinema. Today, the residency of the Diehls is filled from top to bottom with workshops of all kind. Also an appropriate studio, with several adjoining rooms, has been equipped. Only the congenial joint venture of all family members, however, made the creations of the Diehls possible who complement each other in a unique way.

The Diehls originate from an old family of violin-makers. So they unite artistic and mechanic, workmanlike skills in perfect form. The first to find the way to the movies was Ferdinand Diehl, today the reliable director of his puppets. At former *Emelka Company*, he began as scenic painter to end soon after in the animation department. He called in his younger brother Hermann, the creator of the magnificent puppet heads who at that time was art and painting student of Prof. [Angelo] Jank in Munich. After the liquidation of the old *Emelka*, the two decided to go independent. An older brother, grammar school professor Dr. Paul Diehl, joined them as poet, and a first film was developed in 1928/29, the silhouette picture *Caliph Stork*. After this artistic success yet financial failure they had the idea of puppet films. They created the nice supplement films of the *Wupp* series which focused on a little whizz-kid. Six pictures for the old *Bavaria* followed according to scores produced with [Rudolf] Pfenninger's sound system of "Tönende Handschrift" [Sound Handwriting], then five different short films and the feature *The 7 Ravens*. In 1936 they started work on films for education. [...]

Behind these outside stages of development and build-up there is an enormous sum of painstaking and intense work. The basic conditions to produce a puppet film had to be provided and one will notice on a tour through the workshops of the Diehls at every turn all possible inventions in the field of mechanics.

Dr. Paul Diehl was our obliging guide. Himself a teacher, he knows of course about the likes of children and has proved himself a formidable screenwriter. He is an exception among all film writers, because for the peculiarity of the puppet film his screenplays are filmed word for word, syllable for syllable without the slightest change. The puppet film necessitates the production of the soundtrack first, because the mouth movements of the puppets have to be adapted exactly to the previously recorded dialogue. According to the soundtrack the so-called exposure sheet is developed, an ingenious record of each frame of puppet mouth movement. But let's return to our tour. Actually nothing is missing what we have in a "large" movie studio! For instance, the birthplace of the actors: Here we enter the realm of Hermann Diehl. More than 1,000 puppets rest in shelfs. The hands of sculptor Hermann Diehl create always new puppet heads. In another room the bodies are prepared; brass ball-and-socket armatures guarantee unlimited movement. After a puppet actor has been finished, he is transferred to the skilled hands of the Diehls' mother. The old lady wraps the armature in soft cotton, until the projected corpus has been ready which then is being dressed. What the skilful lady accomplishes in this regard would fill a book itself. For *Puss in Boots (Der gestiefelte Kater)* we saw Rokoko ladies and cavaliers in clothes so perfect and stylized as in some of the best historic prestige pictures. Three female assistants work temporarily in dressmaking. In the upper rooms there are more workshops. Here the sets are developed; there they glue, paint, solder, saw, gild, gold-plate and nail everywhere. Here we find true master pieces of painstaking architectonic work. We saw parts of a throne room with real parquet floor; on the abundantly with ornamentation decorated walls miniature paintings. Tables, chairs and other furniture of a bewitching reality. Actually the Diehls are proud to achieve such utter realism in a miniature world. Their team consists of special workers who are fully prepared for their tasks, each a master in his department. 10 to 15 persons are permanently employed in the facilities, and a fourth brother, the painter Robert Diehl from Trier, has joined recently. The house includes a projection, trick and editing room, and one has to admit that nothing is missing what one will find in real film facilities.

Across the residential building with the various workshops is the studio. Here, too, everything is like in "real movies": considerable lighting equipment, torn down and built up sets, various backgrounds and a cyclorama. The studio is very spacious, including a lighting bridge and all kind of tools needed in movies. Right now the outer front of a castle entrance is being made. Unnoticed in a corner of the studio a magnificent golden king's coach is displayed, drawn by two marvellous white horses: a masterpiece of applied arts. The prop shop, a goldmine of arduous artistry, is filled under the roof with sets and props of all kind. More adjoining rooms include the actual joinery and a darkroom laboratory to develop the film strips. This is necessary as a trickfilm consists of too many sources of error which have to be checked immediately. One should imagine what it means to re-adjust 30 to 50 puppets frame by frame! Of course, all cameras have special stop-frame motors, which were invented by the Diehls too.[4]

The puppets of the Diehls usually were about 43 cm [16.9 in.], a quarter of a human. Mimicking expressions and mouth movements were made possible by exchangeable puppet mouth parts. On June 12, 1935, Ferdinand Diehl applied for a patent, "Puppe mit lösbaren auswechselbaren Teilen zur Herstellung von Filmen nach dem Einbildaufnahmeverfahren" [Puppet with soluble, exchangeable parts for film production in stop-frame process, patent no. 404937, Reichspatentamt Berlin].

The audience consisted of soldiers at the front and Hitler Youth at the home front. They were asked to find in these fairy puppet tales a message with a timely meaning. A pupil in the eighth grade who saw the Diehls' version of *Table-Be-Set* (*Tischlein deck dich*) wrote a school essay:

Yesterday, accompanied by much laughter of the undergraduate class, we saw the picture *Table-Be-Set*. For us grown-ups the fairy tale, however, provided more than entertainment and joy, because in every fairy tale there is a deeper meaning. Today we discussed with our teacher the deeper meaning of this fairy tale.

Two tailor's sons acquired, according to the fairy tale, by hard work prosperity and wealth, one in the form of a *Table-Be-Set*, the other in the form of a *Gold-Donkey*. Happily they returned home. But the evil and envious landlord robbed them of prosperity and wealth. Luck seemed to have deserted them.

The third brother, however, put an abrupt end to the fraud of the host through the *Cudgel-out-of-the-sack*. This demonstrates that for the maintenance and security of prosperity and wealth a strong *Wehrmacht* [German military] is necessary, just a Cudgel-out-of-the-sack. It alone is able to regain the lost treasures for the others.

The three sons of the tailor come, as the fairy tale tells us, from Dingsda [Dingbat]. Dingsda, however, is somewhere in Germany, it can be anywhere. So the three brothers represent our whole German nation which has to master life as the three apprentices do. The little goblin, that lives in fairy-tale land and gives the brothers work and pay, represents the luck that everybody needs. For a time it seemed as if luck had abandoned the three good brothers; but then it returns to them forever.

The treacherous host, who hoped to get rich by employing swindle and meanness, faced the fate of punishment. He resembles the eternal Jew who wants to profit from the work of the diligent and capable without moving a single finger. He is a *Schmarotzer* [parasite] who only wants to suck the others and exploit them. In spite of his smartness he can't escape punishment; for there is the Cudgel-out-of-the-sack.

So at the end of our review we have come to the conclusion:

1. By work German people acquire prosperity and wealth.
2. The evil Jew wants to rob the German people of prosperity and wealth.
3. German people, however, secures its prosperity and wealth by a strong army.
4. Only a hard-working nation is lucky in the long run.

So this fairy tale strengthens and invigorates us in our unruly belief in the *Endsieg* [final victory] of Germany in this war. Its "Cudgel-out-of-the-sack" drums heavily on the back of our enemies until all who have called upon the cudgel will buckle like the malicious host did.[5]

REFERENCES

1. *An Animated Dispute: Arthur Melbourne-Cooper and the Birth of Film Animation.* Norwich Film Festival, December 2, 2012.
2. September 1938: Der deutsche Film: *"Poet am Tricktisch"* Besuch bei Starewitsch [The German Film: "Poet at the Animation Stand" Visiting Starevich.]
3. H. O. Schulze quoted from Rolf Giesen, *Der Trickfilm: A Survey of German Special Effects.* In: *Cinefex* No. 25, Riverside/California, 1986.
4. *Gebr. Diehls eigenwillige Kunstschöpfung: Filmatelier ... für Puppen. Eine wohlorganisierte Märchenwelt, von der das Publikum wenig kennt.* [The Diehl Brothers' Idiosyncratic Creation of Art: A Film Studio... for Puppets. A well-organized fairy tale world unknown to the audience.] In: *Der Film.* January 18, 1941.
5. Deutscher Kulturdienst: "Knüppel aus dem Sack" School essay—recorded by Ferdinand Josef Holzer. Collection of J. P. Storm. July 4, 1941.

CHAPTER 4

Puppetoons versus Jiří Trnka

SQUASH AND STRETCH IN WOOD

George Pal, as we have seen, came from cartooning and 2D animation and was the one to transfer the methods and aesthetics of 2D cartoons into dimensional animation.

While producing his first cigarette commercials in Berlin before the Nazi rise to power, Pal had changed sides and switched from flat 2D to dimensional 3D animation, but, contrary to the tardiness of Hermann (puppet maker) and Ferdinand (director-animator) Diehl, he put the dynamics of 2D in it. His artists and technicians, in Eindhoven and later in Hollywood, would create each animated move of a puppet character in wood and replace figures frame by frame, making walking cycles possible as in 2D animation and distorting characters like in 2D's cartoony style. This was Pal's particular *replacement animation*, in short, a mix of 2D and 3D techniques.

It was like *squash and stretch* with puppets. Pal aimed for wacky cartooniness. With his technique, he was able to exaggerate the movements of his puppets into the realm of the caricature.

Therefore, everything, every step, was preplanned and, before any animation was done, carved in wood. The animators' job was to place the puppets, remove heads and extremities, do mouth movements, and other things. Pal was the exact opposite of Starevich. He was no alchemist; he was an industrialist of puppetry who, like Henry Ford, had discovered his own assembly line principles:

> Every animator was given a detailed cue sheet, prepared by Pal, with each movement laboriously illustrated and synchronized to previously recorded music and dialogue. This setup meant that when the foot of a model touched the floor or a facial reaction occurred, the action was perfectly timed to the music. The model builders constructed sectioned boxes holding the various parts of every character, all coded to match the cue sheet. According to the cue sheet, the animator would replace parts of the model in sequence to produce movement.
>
> Pal's meticulous planning was to allow several animators to work on the same sequence without any noticeable variation in style. Hence, the animators were given little room for individual expression, with each move worked out to the smallest detail on the precise cue sheets. The system only occasionally allowed "freehand" animation [...][1]

The Europeans loved Pal's Puppetoons, as they were later called, but wouldn't stick with this tradition. His system was clearly devised for America. But in Hollywood exile, Pal's cartoons were among many others and, although three-dimensional, not different from Terrytoons or Walter Lantz's work. Even his American distributor, Paramount Pictures, released the 2D *Popeye* series in competition with their client Pal.

Two animation artists from Buenos Aires, Alberto Couceiro and Alejandra Tomei, are the only filmmakers I know in Germany who are still, with certain modifications, on George Pal's track.

Alejandra Tomei. (Courtesy of Animas Film.)

I asked them what the challenge was in working physically with puppets and not with all those digital tools.

Alejandra Tomei: I like the real world most, the world of objects, a world that is haptic, a world that you can touch. This is the place where I feel well, about which I can talk most.

Every man-made object has its story, an existence that talks to me. These objects have their own logic. The objects, which we create in our studio, eventually develop their own "soul" which we try to understand. The challenge is to share these stories through our films with other people.

Alberto Couceiro: Stop motion is one of the oldest techniques in cinematography. It combines various other techniques.

To create armatures for instance one must gain expertise in metal working and for the puppet construction you need to combine a lot of materials. The task to build sets and models is a world of its own. Then there is the traditional craftsmanship like photography and lighting and now we got digital image processing.

Alberto Couceiro. (Courtesy of Animas Film.)

In all these fields we have to experiment, master each technique, we have to know the various materials to produce a result of high quality. This is one of the challenges working with puppets and working physically. It's real handiwork in a world which as a result of digitalization becomes more and more abstract and incomprehensible.

For independent artists and filmmakers it is a great obligation to maintain and develop all these techniques more or less under one roof.

We are moving into a wide and open world of objects for which you need time and space, a scarce commodity in our era.

Alejandra Tomei readily admits that digital techniques and digital photography have opened up enormous new possibilities for stop motion: Small and light equipment is sufficient to shoot high-quality images. You get the result at once. You can process the images in different ways and much more… We are able to work spontaneously and use our intuition.

Alberto Couceiro: Surprise is the fascinating and magical part about animation. The unexpected is what makes animation special. One cannot easily reproduce these moments. Puppet play and movements are being built in one session, a scene in a few hours, in front of the camera, frame by frame. It depends on many other factors. It is a "live-play" which takes place between animator and figure, and the whole movement can be seen several hours after single-frame shooting. Then it's the details that determine beauty and charm. One is always looking for such moments. It's a subtle perception. You cannot say why a certain animation scene is beautiful. The reason must be that is has the certain something that is so hard to describe. It's always these tiny details that make us recognize life and charm. This is our motivation to go on and animate and bring these figures to life: to look for a human character and find yourself.

TÝRLOVÁ AND ZEMAN

After the war, the center of European puppet animation was Czechoslovakia.

In the small city of Zlín, in Socialist times to become Gottwaldov, an old shoe factory was transformed into an animation studio. Animators and technicians were occasionally commissioned by the German occupants and specialized in puppet animation. There was an ongoing competition in that studio between Hermína Týrlová and her former animator Karel Zeman.

Týrlová was born on December 11, 1900, in Březové Hory u Příbrami, and died on May 3, 1993, in Zlín. She came from a mining company and during her childhood had lost both parents. Hermína started as an actress, the same as Lotte Reiniger, but her husband, Karel Dodal, was so fascinated by the American

Alberto Couceiro animating *TV City*, which won the Third Prize of the Cinefondation at the 56th Cannes Film Festival in 2003. (Courtesy of Animas Film.)

Puppets from *Automatic Fitness*, a 2015 short film produced by Alberto Couceiro and Alejandra Tomei. (Courtesy of Animas Film.)

cartoons, particularly by Max Fleischer's *Out of the Inkwell* series, that his wife began to focus on animation in the late 1920s. In 1936, Týrlová changed to puppet animation. During the war, she chose a popular newspaper character, Ferda the Ant, and transformed him into a dimensional puppet. In her postwar *Rebellion of Toys* (*Vzpoura hraček*), she had puppets unite and force a Nazi soldier to flee. The film won Best Children's Film at the festival in Venice and Best Puppet Film at the festival in Brussels.

Týrlová's former associate Zeman, born on November 3, 1910, in Ostroměř, Austria-Hungary, would go another way. He had studied at a French advertising school and until 1936 worked for an advertising company in Marseille. It was here that he encountered animation when he did an advertising film for soap. He was quite the polyglot and therefore always would strive for intercultural, not Czech, topics. His cameraman, Antonín Horák, with whom I corresponded for some time shortly before his death, blamed Zeman for not focusing on national Slavic topics. The reason was that Zeman had visited Morocco, Egypt, Yugoslavia, and Greece and inhaled foreign cultures and styles. Having returned to his home country, Czechoslovakia, and doing advertising films, unable to leave the country during German occupation, he was introduced by a fellow filmmaker named Elmar Klos to the Bata puppet film studio in the Kudlov suburb in Zlín, where he was invited to join Týrlová's unit.

On his own, Zeman created the character of Pan Pokouk, an "animated cousin" of Jacques Tati's Monsieur Hulot, and also made a lovely color short, *Inspirace,* with animated glass figurines in 1949.

Having finished his first feature-length puppet film, *The Treasure of Bird Island* (*Poklad ptačího*), which was inspired by Persian paintings, in 1953, Zeman went into a genre that would mix live-action, puppet, and model animation, as well as 2D animation, and create a rather stylized, completely synthetic type of movie. The first film of this kind was still rather conventional: the Agfacolor *Journey to the Beginning of Time* (*Cesta do pravěku*), released in 1955, which sent a group of boys to the age of the dinosaurs. The scenes with the boys were filmed previously; then, by using a split screen, the 50-cm rubber puppets were added in postproduction.

Zeman's most ambitious feature, which went over schedule and budget, was *The Fabulous World of Jules Verne* (*Vynález zkázy*), which allowed him to enter the fantastic world of French utopian Jules Verne:

> One of the central problems in the acceptance of films such as this *[The Fabulous World of Jules Verne]* is that Americans have trained Hollywood to give them films with lots of special effects, and Hollywood has responded with films in the mode of stylization called "realism." That is, effects that always are *supposed* to look as if they were happening in reality. Actually, that's not quite what it is. Hollywood gives us heightened, interpreted "reality": spaceships that roar in the airless vacuum of space and bank like fighter planes against the resistance of air that isn't there; floods that tower above buildings like waves instead of welling up around them; waves at sea that are higher than ships; dinosaurs that behave like crabby lizards... What Zeman did in *The Fabulous World of Jules Verne* was simple, yet objected by many moviegoers: he tried to bring to life on screen the style of illustrations that accompanied the first editions of Verne's works.[2]

This type of stylization, to imitate the original wood engravings or line block reproductions of the books, won prizes all around after the movie's release in 1958 but was not considered "realistic" by many moviegoers. According to Zeman's trick cameraman Antonín Horák, there was a simple technical reason for it: all effects had to be done by latent image in a Czech Šlechta camera (named after its engineer, Josef Šlechta) on the original negative. The composites, therefore, jiggled slightly. Šlechta's camera was nothing compared to the Mitchell models, but thanks to foreground glasses with horizontal lines cleverly arranged by Horák, you wouldn't detect the technical faults:

> This complicated marriage of live-action, drawings and puppet-like models meant that the same film strip went through the camera three or four times, for example, for some scenes cartoons were first drawn of the outdoor backgrounds. Then a weird, 12-propeller flying machine—actually a two-foot long plastic miniature—was photographed via the puppet stop-action method, superimposed over the same film. Then live actors, filmed in appropriate perspective, went through their paces, and this was superimposed again over the drawings and puppet-type miniatures.[3]

Zeman's stylized works became an influence to a selected number of filmmakers, including Tim Burton and Terry Gilliam, who wanted his sadly failed *Munchausen* epic to be more of an homage to Zeman's Gustave Doré-styled *The Fabulous Baron Munchausen* (*Baron Prášil*), not to the Nazi-*Munchausen* made in 1942.

THE TRICK BROTHERS

The largest number of Czech animators, however, assembled in Prague. When WWII was over, a group of highly effective 2D artists who had worked under German occupation changed, like Pal had done, to 3D puppets, but in a completely different style.

Jiří Trnka, the new rising star of the Prague animation scene, didn't work with comic strips like George Pal but with illustrations-turned-puppets. During the war he had illustrated children's books. People refer to him sometimes as "Walt Disney of the East." He definitely was not. Trnka pleaded not for naturalism but for stylization of the scenery, an artificially heroic look for the human actors, and lyrical content of the theme.

Trnka's ambition was to move three-dimensional figures of puppets in space, the same as Jürgen Clausen had demanded, and in contradistinction to the heroes of 2D cartoons. From the beginning, he said, he had his own conception of how puppets could be handled. Each of them should have an individual but static facial expression, as compared with the puppets that by means of various technical devices could change their mien in an attempt to achieve a more life-like aspect. In practice, this hadn't enhanced realism but had rather been conducive to naturalism.

The puppets in Trnka's short and feature films would act just by movement and body stance. George Pal's replacement animation was totally different, just the contrary in pacing and character.

Trnka was born on February 24, 1912, in Pilsen. As a young man, he became interested in puppets and puppet play. He liked art and learned to enjoy puppet making from his grandmother. Early on in his hometown, he got in touch with Josef Skupa, the creator of the *Spejbl and Hurvínek* father and son marionettes. From 1929 until 1935, Trnka attended the Prague School of Arts and Crafts and started a puppet theater of his own. After the war, he became involved in the Prague animation studio, *Bratri v Triku* (*Trick Brothers*), and after some anti-Fascist 2D animation (*The Chimney Sweep/Springman & the SS/Pérák a SS*) turned the group to puppets and short and feature-length stop motion.

Contrary to Zeman, Trnka was very Czech in style and narration: the delightful *Czech Year* (*Špaliček*), the fairy tale *Prince Bayaya* (*Bajaja*), *Old Czech Legends* (*Staré povesti české*), and *The Good Soldier Svejk* (*Dobrý voják Švejk*). He also did Anton Chekov (*Story of a Bass/Román s basou*), a spoof on John Ford's *Stagecoach* (*Song of the Prairie/Árie prérie*), Hans Christian Andersen (*The Emperor's Nightingale/Císařův slavík*), and his masterpiece, a puppet version of Shakespeare's *A Midsummer Night's Dream* (*Sen noci svatojánské*) in color and scope (four-track stereo). The Czech officials hoped it would win the Golden Palm (*Palme d'Or*) at the Cannes Film Festival in 1959, but when it didn't, the *Literature Paper* of the Czech Writers' Association criticized Trnka's venture into Shakespeare: *With this Trnka has entered a field on which he hadn't worked before. The* Midsummer Night's Dream *isn't close to our people, and Trnka didn't try to make it acceptable to us; he rather would keep the Shakespearean English character of his figures and symbols.*

Trnka continued to make more puppet films, including the anti-Stalinist, anti-personality cult *The Hand (Ruka)*, in which a giant hand is going to brainwash a harlequin potter not to make flower vases, just statues of The Hand, but he didn't do any more puppet features. After Trnka's death on December 30, 1969, the little movie was banned for some time.

DISNEY PLUS BUŇUEL AND CHARLES BOWERS

Although he didn't exactly continue Trnka's tradition, Jan Švankmajer is today the most influential Czech stop-motion animator. He is in a class of his own and totally surrealist (similar to the work of the Quay Brothers). The late Milos Forman described Švankmayer as "Disney plus Buňuel." Both Trnka and Švankmajer were declared anti-Stalinists. In *The Death of Stalinism in Bohemia (Konec stalinismu w Čzechách)*, Stalin's bust is opened on an operating table to reveal (in animation) Czech history from 1948 to 1989:

> Švankmajer's cinematic worlds are startling. Clay humanoids melt and transform. Household objects, vegetables, raw meat, and animal parts spring to life. Live actors become stop-motion puppets and life-size marionettes. Whether a poetic short or a plot-driven feature, his films are simultaneously playful and grim, hopeful and cynical.[4]

Švankmajer was born in Prague on September 4, 1934, the same year the Czech Surrealist Group was formed. His experimental films are a mélange of puppets, live-action, collage, drawn animation, clay, and object animation.

Švankmajer once compared himself to Charles Bowers (1889–1946), an artist-turned-comedian or comedian-turned-artist:

> The first time I saw Bowers' films was in the Seventies, even after I had completed my first film *The Flat*. There

are two Bowers films in the Czech Film Archive. After the director of this archive saw my films, he contacted me and said "I have something here that you might be interested in." So I went down and saw the films, and I realized that he was my predecessor in what I was doing, because he was mixing animation and live-action 50 years before I started filmmaking. But we are talking in terms of technique, not content.[5]

I had the chance to screen some Bowers footage at the Berlin International Film Festival in February 1985 and saw it in the presence of Dennis Muren, one of the greatest visual effects (VFX) experts in the history of films. We both were stunned by what Bowers had achieved in *Egged On*. It's about a machine that turns ordinary, breakable eggs into rubbery, unbreakable ones for transport, a process that unreels a huge amount of surrealist stop-motion effects.

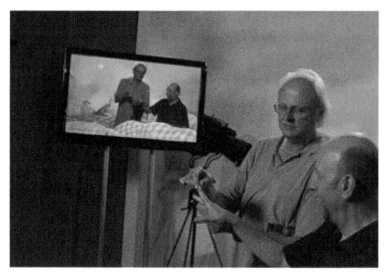

Dennis Muren tries to animate the author while visiting Filmpark Babelsberg in July 2010. (Courtesy of Filmpark Babelsberg.)

In his surrealistic slapstick world, Bowers starred stop-motion objects in an animation process that was his own invention. It was a marriage of slapstick and animation: *eggs hatch Ford automobiles, a Christmas tree grows out of a farmer, a mouse shoots a cat with a revolver, Charley grows a bush which in turn sprouts cats, etc. etc.*[6]

Later Charles Bowers was involved in a color short, *Pete Roleum and His Cousins*, that was directed by Joseph Losey, scored by Hanns Eisler, and presented at the 1938–1939 New York's World Fair. His coanimator on the picture was Lou Bunin.

LOU IN WONDERLAND

Bunin was not born in America. He was born in Kiev on February 17, 1904, which made him a true advocate of puppet films. Bunin ran a marionette theater in Chicago, before he discovered the world of "stringless" marionettes: stop-motion puppets. In 1942, Bunin came down to Hollywood, where he did inserts and special effects for the big studios and did an animated prologue for MGM's star-studded *Ziegfeld Follies*. But for his plan of a feature-length stop-motion film, Bunin was unable to secure any backing in the United States. To accomplish the venture of a feature-length puppet version of *Alice in Wonderland*, with a live Alice (Carol Marsh) in the prologue, he had to go to Europe, to France.

> *Lou Bunin*: We started in 1949… It was released in '51, and over one million dollars was spent on it. We made two versions—one French and one English. I feel I did *Lewis Carroll's Alice in Wonderland*, while the Disney version was a sort of *Mickey Mouse in Wonderland*. He disregarded whole portions of the book, rewriting to suit his own needs. My version didn't make too much money, but it paid everybody back and made a little profit. […] Disney wanted me to hold my picture in storage for three years,

to let him exploit his film first...so that my one million dollar picture wouldn't benefit from the much larger advertising campaign he'd planned for his three million dollar picture. But I opened my picture first, and when he took me to court over this the judge threw the case out. He stated that since *Alice* was in the public domain, anyone could do a version of it, and that there had already been four feature-length films of it done previously. Nearly everyone said that Disney's *Alice* suffered by comparison to mine, and that we were much truer to Carroll's original story. [...]

There were eighty people involved in the production of *Alice in Wonderland*. All of the animation was done in a big studio in France. We had wonderful workmen making props—the Hall of Doors, the trees, the garden sets.

HANSEL AND GRETEL

The first to succeed in producing a feature-length puppet film in the United States was Michael Myerberg, a native of Baltimore. To the theater world, Myerberg was no unknown, but regarding films and puppets, he was a stranger. His stage productions included stars like Fredric March, Tallulah Bankhead, and Yul Brynner. He also managed the Philadelphia Ballet. He had helped to produce the soundtrack for *100 Men and a Girl* with Deanna Durbin and conductor Leopold Stokowski. Stokowski went on to join Walt Disney and *Fantasia*; Myerberg followed in Disney's footsteps when the producer of Mickey Mouse left his distribution company, RKO. RKO, in need of an animated product for Christmas release in 1954, decided in favor of Myerberg's version of Engelbert Humperdinck's opera *Hansel and Gretel*, the first animated feature to be produced in New York City, at Myerberg's Second Avenue Studio, located at 216 East 2nd St., between Avenue B and Avenue C. It was announced as having been produced with puppets controlled by electrical solenoids, so-called *kinemins,* which, of course, was a "closely-guarded trade secret" only as far as promotion was concerned. Actually, *Hansel and Gretel* was ordinary stop motion, as the late Don Sahlin, one of the puppeteers-turned-animators who worked on the show, recalled:

> The only thing "electronic" was the electromagnetic setup that held the puppets on the stage. Myerberg had a big panel upstairs where he'd use close-up heads that were wired to this big, blinking board. You'd turn knobs, but there was nothing electronic involved. There was simply a wire inside the mouth, and with a twist of a certain knob, the mouth would go "that way," and so on. But it was all manual. Anything else that was said was a big put-on.[7]

The elaborate puppets were one-third life-size and cost $2500 apiece to make.

MEMORY HOTEL

For many years now, Berlin-based stop-motion artist Heinrich Sabl, technically working not in replacement of but more or less in Trnka's stop-motion style, albeit not as filigree as Trnka, not for children, has been tilting at windmills like a modern-day Don Quixote and trying to finish a feature-length adult stop-motion film, *Memory Hotel*:

> While I was trained as a puppeteer back in the 1980s the puppet play tried to emancipate, and this was underlined by some theoretical work, for instance by Konstanza Kavrakova Lorenz. Puppetry discovered the adult audience. And we understood "the puppet" as our tool— as a material which, depending on the story, could be replaced through other materials which includes an actor. In the process of work with the material a terminology

Heinrich Sabl animates a puppet under the open sky. (Courtesy of Heinrich Sabl.)

was established that has since accompanied my work. The lifeless material (it might be a thing, it might be a puppet) becomes a character by means of animation. In this regard the term puppet doesn't exist for me. It is just material, a tool that transforms by the process of animation/life giving into a character. A figure with regard to screenplay/the literary source, however, that ceases the right to be a character if we, the recipients, won't believe in it.

When I animate I have to embrace the material. In the material I find all information for the camerawork, the choreography and, related to that, the animation.

To work with puppets is a question of matter. It's a haptic thing, all about touching metal, wood, rubber. But it's certainly not about photo-realism.

Scenes from the upcoming feature-length *Memory Hotel* that span a production history of 15 years. (Courtesy of Heinrich Sabl.)

REFERENCES

1. Mike Hankin, *Ray Harryhausen: Master of the Majicks, Volume 1: Beginnings and Endings.* Los Angeles: Archive Editions, 2013, p. 199.
2. Bill Warren, *Keep Watching the Skies!* Volume II. Jefferson, NC, and London: McFarland & Company, 1986, pp. 511–512.
3. Alan Mobley, *American Cinematographer,* October 1958.
4. Eoin Koepfinger, "Freedom Is Becoming the Only Theme": An Interview with Jan Švankmajer. *Sampsonia Way,* June 5, 2012. http://www.sampsoniaway.org.
5. Wendy Jackson, The Surrealist Conspirator: An Interview with Jan Svankmajer. *Animation World Magazine* (23), June 1997.
6. *Charles R. Bowers, or The Marriage of Slapstick and Animation.* November 22, 1983. https://bampfa.org/event/charles-r-bowers-or-marriage.slapstick-and-animation
7. Don Sahlin interviewed by David Prestone for *Closeup Magazine,* no. 2, 1976.

CHAPTER 5

The Dynamators

M ANY OUTSTANDING VFX ARTISTS involved with some of the great blockbusters of our days confirm the influence of stop-motion animator Ray Harryhausen (1920–2013), not because he was working in animation but because of his special technique of compositing and having model animation interact with live-action photography, like his mentor, Willis O'Brien, did in the silent *Lost World* (1925) and the original *King Kong* (1933).

THE LOST WORLD

The Lost World dioramas were actually populated by 49 foam rubber dinosaurs with jointed armatures. Outtakes prove that O'Brien worked with several other animators and didn't do the animation all by himself. While *The Lost World* was in production, famous visitors to the set included Charles Chaplin and German film director Fritz Lang on his first trip to the United States: *They saw brontosauri which were a foot high and towered above miniature forests. Twelve cameras were employed in taking one frame at a time of this picture, and often the director only made a few feet of film a week, each slightest movement of the animal miniatures having to receive the most careful technical attention. Mr. Lang referred to this production as a technical masterpiece.*[1]

THE "ZEUS COMPLEX"

Young Harryhausen assisted Willis O'Brien on the animation of *Mighty Joe Young*: *When I start a scene I know the broad outline but not the details. They come to you as you're animating.*[2] The animator must have felt like God. Harryhausen always joked about his "Zeus Complex".

I asked film historian Mike Hankin, who has devoted three enormous volumes of *Master of the Majicks* to the work of Harryhausen and his so-called *Dynamation* entries: Do you see an evolution from Ray's films to present-day computer-generated imagery (CGI)?

> *Mike answered*: Many of today's practitioners in CGI confess to being influenced and to reference Ray's work. If there is a need to create an apparent living being, the portrayal of accurate movement is paramount to maintain believability. Ray was a master of the

The author joins Ray Harryhausen in the village church of Harriehausen not far away from Hanover. (Courtesy of Stefan Birckmann.)

Ray Harryhausen (r.) never encountered the star of his first solo feature-length creature movie *The Beast from 20,000 Fathoms* way back in 1952. Finally, the two "dinosaurs," Ray and Swiss-born Paul Christian, a.k.a. Paul Hubschmid, met in Berlin at the opening of the Film Museum in 2000. The author and the late Arnold Kunert smile in the background. (Courtesy of Stefan Birckmann.)

movement, perfected over years of careful study and countless experimentation. His method of creating this movement through model animation may now be seen as outdated, at least as far as supposedly living creatures are concerned, but how they moved is still a specialized skill. CGI is only a progression of technique. I have little doubt that the thousands of film industry artists in the past that built, painted, manipulated images and all the other skills that combine to make moving pictures would have loved to use today's technology if it had been available to them. In reverse, many of the people who presently work in the industry yearn for the tactile satisfaction of creating something by hand. The sad fact is that in most cases the public will not accept less than perfect effects. The destruction of obvious miniatures, hand-painted backdrops, objects held aloft by wires and, dare I say it, creatures created through the use of model

The griffin and the centaur in a fighting mood in an exhibition staged at Filmpark Babelsberg. (Courtesy of Filmpark Babelsberg GmbH.)

animation are now regarded with a degree of derision. The public can still enjoy and admire films made with physical effects in the past, but in a sort of tolerant, nostalgic way.

Mike is also an expert on George Pal and the Puppetoons studio where Ray Harryhausen started his professional career: I think a line can be drawn between the influence of the George Pal puppet films and the genus of film with which Ray Harryhausen is associated. One of the reasons that Ray came up with the name Dynamation was to differentiate his type of film to that of drawn or pure puppet animation. The characters in Pal's Puppetoon films were never meant to be viewed as living entities, whereas the Harryhausen creatures were intended to be part of the real world. The lines did cross, with Ray producing his pure animated puppet fairy tale films at the beginning of his career and Pal using single animated figures that were meant to be living creatures, such as the squirrel in *The Great Rupert* (1949) and the Loch Ness Monster in *7 Faces of Dr. Lao* (1964), but in general they were known for differing types of animated figures. Shades of Pal's Puppetoons can be seen in CGI films such as the *Toy Story* series, although the humor is vastly different. The influence of Harryhausen permeates everything from *Jurassic Park* (1993) to *Avatar* (2009) and beyond.*

I recall having tried to get a series off the ground titled *Ray Harryhausen's World of Myth and Legend*. It was our intention to have Ray introduce legends from all over the world, from Greek mythology to *Ilya Muromets* and Japanese ghost stories, and illustrate the narration with puppet films. After a while, giving it thought, Ray refused to continue that way and said it had to be Dynamation topics, models composited with live action, not 100 percent puppet animation. He never thought of his films as puppet films but as VFX productions. *This is what we are identified with*, he said, and defined it as his trademark. This meant that the puppet film approach was out and VFX were in, but eventually the project was not killed for reasons of VFX. Green screen and VFX plates were state of the art; the animation was not.

Jim Danforth, the other great American stop-motion artist who is usually associated with VFX (Academy Award nominations for *7 Faces of Dr. Lao* and *When Dinosaurs Ruled the Earth*), was much more interested in puppetry and regular puppet films than Ray, and named among his favorites Trnka's puppet *Midsummer Night's Dream* and Japanese animator Kihachirō Kawamoto, who had been trained under Tadahito Mochinaga and Trnka himself. It is a shame that Danforth couldn't prove his artistry in that field by the production of proposed stop-motion versions of Stravinsky's *Firebird* and *Siegfried*.

---

* The living skeletons in Tim Burton's *Miss Peregrine's Home for Peculiar Children* (2016).

Jim Danforth's sculpture of Prince Ivan would have appeared in a stop-motion version of *The Firebird*. (Courtesy of Jim Danforth.)

Many of the younger generation of VFX artists were inspired as kids by Harryhausen and tried to copy him later. One of those youngsters, Dennis Muren, who went to see Harryhausen's *7th Voyage of Sinbad* eight times during its first week in 1958, wasn't very fond of his own experiments with stop motion. So he became a cameraman and had to photograph the stop-motion animation of other youngsters like David Allen and Phil Tippett, which must have been rather tiring and depressing. Eventually, Dennis found a way to substitute frame-by-frame stop-motion animation with more lifelike, kinetic GC animation and, most importantly, he didn't need the advice of computer scientists anymore while animating.

Another of Jim's unfinished stop-motion dreams: *Siegfried.*
Here Wotan is shown in front of a waterfall. (Courtesy of
Jim Danforth.)

AT THE CRADLE OF THE DIGITAL AGE—AND NOT KNOWING IT

So, unintentionally, Ray Harryhausen stood at the cradle of the
digital age in cinematography. His Dynamation composites of
live action and puppets made people think to just substitute the
puppets to make the effect of animation more fluid.

When Ray Harryhausen first saw scenes from Disney's
Dinosaurs (2000), it was not the lifelike animation or the creatures'
textures he noticed but the sheer number of dinosaurs involved
in certain scenes, while he himself had only four of them in *The
Valley of Gwangi* (1969). Concerning the movements, however, he
didn't notice that many differences from his own approach from
previous days. Nevertheless, these *Dinosaurs*, as typical for Disney,
were humanized like they would do in a cartoon, in *The Land
Before Time* series—which Harryhausen wouldn't have dared.
King Kong, yes, but dinosaurs?

Ray Harryhausen's *Gwangi* was inspired by an ill-fated project developed by his mentor Willis H. O'Brien in the 1940s. (Courtesy of Filmpark Babelsberg GmbH.)

Otherwise, Harryhausen echoed what we said: CGI has its virtues as a tool, but they hype it to the point where everything else should be discarded which I don't agree with. Thunderbirds brought back string puppets, Kermit the Frog brought back hand puppets which go back to ancient Rome. So it depends on the story you're telling. Some techniques are better than others for certain types of stories. [...] On a fantasy film I think it defeats the point if you try to make it too realistic. Half the charm of *King Kong* was that it was like a nightmare. You couldn't believe your eyes. You knew it wasn't real and yet it looked real. [...] Motion pictures have become so inundated in our society over the years. Stop motion adds something to a fantasy film whereas with CGI, I could never see the point of making everything too real, unless you're making, you know, a special documentary about something. The BBC made *Walking with Dinosaurs* and that was beautifully done. But that was a different thing. I think when you're

Jim Danforth on the track of stop-motion entomologist Ladislas Starevich: the puppets of Billy Bee and fiddling Gypsy Cricket were created several years prior to the release of either A *Bug's Life* or *Antz*. (Courtesy of Jim Danforth.)

making a melodrama or a subject depending on fantasy subjects, if you make it too real you lose, you defeat the point, you bring it down to the mundane.[3]

As it is with everything else that is very special, stop motion definitely depends on the art of true master craftsmen. Early in the 1960s, Disney was setting up a small department for stop motion. In his memoir, Jim Danforth tells an incredible story of how these people did a lot of research to have puppets stand upright. They put them on glass or whatever and didn't consult any expert but proved to themselves that puppets will fall and so discontinued the experiment![4]

REFERENCES

1. Mike Hankin, *Ray Harryhausen: Master of the Majicks, Volume 1: Beginnings and Endings.* Los Angeles: Archive Editions, 2013, p. 199. Reprinted by permission of the author.
2. Rick Trembles, "God Complex," Hallowed by Thy Name! An Interview with Ray Harryhausen. *Offscreen*, 9(8), September 2005.
3. Rick Trembles, "God Complex." *Offscreen*, 9(8), September 2005 FanTasia 2005 Special.
4. Jim Danforth, *Dinosaurs, Dragons & Drama: The Odyssey of a Trickfilmmaker.* Los Angeles: Archive Editions, 2011.

CHAPTER 6

Pixilation and Mocap

People Become Puppets

NEIGHBOURS AT WAR

Pixilation is an exciting stop-frame technique by which live actors are animated exactly like stop-motion puppets.

One of the undisputed masters of the process was Norman McLaren (1914–1987), who used it to great advantage in the Academy Award–winning satire *Neighbours*, produced in 1952 by the National Film Board of Canada.

McLaren discovered that one can not only animate objects frame by frame but real people, too. He and his colleague Grant Munro started to experiment with the idea. For three days, they shot a series of technical tests that involved 20 seconds of animation of two men fighting. When they viewed the rushes, they saw that the process worked for humans. Even more, McLaren felt that the fighting scene contained a whole story. Two animators, Munro and Jean-Paul Ladouceur, star as peaceful *Neighbours* who, at the height of the Korean War, come into conflict with each other over a flower that blooms between their adjacent cardboard houses. Wolf Koenig handled the photography and McLaren directed, but it would be Munro who termed the process *pixilation* (from *pixilated*).

People shot in this way move in a strange, jerky, stilted, almost surreal way, as if they were puppets manipulated by an unseen force. The physical laws and forces of weight and gravity seem to be neutralized.

One of the gems of the genre is a tour-de-force pixilation starring animator Mike Jittlov that became part of the feature film *The Wizard of Speed and Time.* Pixilation, although done frame by frame, seems to be absolutely spontaneous and grows in action like a slapstick comedy while doing it, in front of as well as behind the camera.

Even in the days of digital animation, this technique is not forgotten. In 2011, Juan Pablo Zaramella, a filmmaker from Buenos Aires, used pixilation for his short film *Luminaris*, which imagines a world controlled by light: a young man (Gustavo Cornillón, who cowrote the script) who works in a factory that produces light bulbs tries to break out from this slave system.

In pixilation, you can create and fill a physical universe of the impossible with its own logic, rich in visual metaphors. And, above all, you can master and change space and time.

AVATAR

A "quantum jump" from Norman McLaren to James Cameron and *Avatar?* Not exactly.

In the days of silent films, by using the process of rotoscoping, animation pioneer Max Fleischer transformed his younger brother Dave into the 2D shape of Koko the Clown, who would have all sorts of adventures in real-life settings. At the beginning of each cartoon, Max was shown dipping his pen into an inkwell, and right *out of the inkwell,* Koko would emerge and jump off the drawing board. The hand of the artist in this case was like the hand of God, and some of today's computer animators might feel likewise. (Disney rotoscoped too, but he would use that live-action footage only as reference for his animators.)

The digital equivalent of rotoscoping and pixilation is motion or performance capture: *mocap.*

Joe Letteri at Weta Digital in New Zealand is one of its undisputed masters. He worked on *Lord of the Rings, Avatar,* and its inevitable sequels:

> The goal of the process is to capture everything the actor is doing and the emotions actors are expressing through their performance. The tools and workflow are designed to make sure the actor is uninhibited and can stay in the moment. Any actor's approach or technique can work in a motion capture context.
>
> Performance capture is far less polarising than it was, in part because artists now have a broader understanding of the process. The data that is gathered through the performance capture process is a starting point for animators to craft a performance. Nothing is determined by the data.
>
> Even when the creative decision is made to replicate an actor's performance with a digital character, there is a tremendous amount of talent and skill that goes into translating the nuances of a human performance onto a digital character that, in most cases, does not share the same physical characteristics.
>
> Performance capture is an additive process; it gives the animator another tool to work with. Traditionally, the animator must rely only on his/her eyes to match reference. Performance capture gives animators a representation of motion that may include subtlety of movement or a slight asymmetry of posture or gait that add to what we perceive subconsciously. Sometimes we don't know why something looks "right," only that it does. In some cases, performance capture can help you get there more quickly by doing the basic work more efficiently, freeing the animator to spend more time polishing that extra 10% that can make a performance.

It's not only freeing the animator. It binds him or her fast to the digital age. *Mocap* actually transforms humans into digital marionettes to serve naturalism in movement and animation.

CHAPTER 7

The Road to Computer-Generated Imagery

THE FORM AND THE SUBSTANCE

Many 2D animators remained skeptical when computers were introduced. Decades ago, Tony White, a British Academy Award-winning animator, wrote:

> Without the varied idiosyncrasies of a human personality, the computer is incapable of giving a living spirit to its creations, and this is the secret ingredient of all great animation. As long as audiences continue to want subtle, sophisticated, and entertaining character animation—where we actually believe that the drawings we see are alive and real—then the role of drawn animation in filmmaking is assured.[1]

Tony made that statement more than 20 years ago and today might regret it, as he has been proven wrong. To the great disappointment of fundamentalist 2D animators, 3D has become the standard. There still is a lot of 2D, particularly in Japan, but the mass has transformed three-dimensionally. We are literally swamped by it. Unlike 2D, the mass of 3D animation is never individual. 2D is more individual. It isn't changed that much after the artist has done a scene. Three-dimensional, on the other hand, can easily be changed during production—details, gestures, facial expressions—and so is based on committee decisions.

Above all, there is one main difference between traditional film and CGI: for film, the content is decisive: the content of photography or the play that is depicted in moving images.

With CGI, it's not necessarily the content, not the substance, and it's not—as Ray Harryhausen had hoped for—the story. It's (to quote Marshall McLuhan) the medium itself. The content is less important than the fascination with the technological gimmicks that sometimes absorb and even "devour" the viewer. They certainly "devour" the artist who becomes one with the digital "universe," because it's more than tools. It is cult.

Jim Danforth was right when he wrote that the traditional animators were more into story:

> The prevailing wisdom in Hollywood is that CGI technology has made stop motion obsolete. Is this good news or bad news? It depends on one's perspective.
>
> Animators like Willis O'Brien, Ray Harryhausen, and Jim Danforth (if I may be permitted to include myself) were motivated primarily by a desire to create stories or sequences or performances through the use of the animation process. Their skills in animation were developed, not because they wanted to find jobs as animators, but because they had something to say.
>
> During the making of traditional stop-motion creature films such as *Mighty Joe Young, The Golden Voyage of Sinbad*, or *When Dinosaurs Ruled the Earth*, the animator is both an actor in, and the director of, the animated scene.

Sometimes the actor is also the writer of the scene or even of the entire film story. The animator may also be the producer of the film.

The studios like CGI because it eliminates many of the union problems that made stop motion almost impossible to do under major studio contracts.

Is there any downside to CGI? I think there is. When I was directing the effects for *Caveman*, the writer/director asked me to do scenes of the dinosaurs defecating.

Those scenes do not appear in *Caveman* because I refused to do them. Today, such a refusal would be meaningless; the director would use CGI to get what he wanted.

In my opinion, the major stop-motion animators have had a civilizing effect on the films on which they have worked. Most directors see animators as meddlers who are diluting the director's vision (and DGA rules enforce that viewpoint).

There was probably more money spent on the CG effects for *Jurassic Park* than was spent on *all* the stop-motion effects ever done in the history of stop motion, so we are comparing apples to raisins. It is interesting to contemplate what might have been accomplished if a courageous producer had managed to provide the same kind of enormous financial support for a stop-motion creature film. Of course, such a large investment would bring with it additional studio oversight, resulting in the suppression of the creative inspiration of the animators.

This then is the significance of stop motion. The lower costs of the process compared to CGI permits individual or small-group creativity to flourish.[2]

Visually, 3D or computer animation is related to stop motion because it's dimensional. In this, it really seems to make stop motion obsolete. But in execution and possibilities for overcoming gravity,

Jim Danforth is an accomplished puppet film animator with a broad variety of projects that include naturalistic and stylized puppets. The maquettes of Jorn and Jorinda were created for a short pantomime film project called *Fable*: Jorn, an inventor, helps Jorinda, a girl from across the river, escape to his free community of artists. (Courtesy of Jim Danforth.)

it's next to 2D and totally different from stop motion. Referring to 2D animation, however, CG images are not as innocent as *Felix the Cat* and his heirs:

> Felix the Cat, for instance, can roll his tail into a wheel and ride off on it as if it were a bicycle. In another case, Felix loses his tail. He wonders what to do and while he ponders a question mark grows out of his head. Felix seizes it and sticks it on his rump. There you go. These images are absolute. There is no difference between appearance and reality.[3]

In 3D computer animation, characters are not subjected to a world of drawn lines on a piece of paper. Thanks to nonlinear interpolation, 3D animation is smooth and fluid, with no sign of frame-by-frame jerkiness. There are no drawn lines anymore and certainly no piece of paper. It's not so much stylized animation, it is realistic *simulation*. These images do not necessarily come from art, they come from industry.

Concerning the characters, there is a lot of building and rigging to be done, but imagery, camera angles, movement, and editing certainly have the quality of live-action, and in some cases, the characters already look like us. We begin to accept them as equals.

Digital media make the simulation of nonexistent realistic worlds a daily affair. It's an incredible world of make-believe. The objective is not to copy our sensuous and physical experience but the image of it. Eventually, it will become the world dominion of imagery, with digitization and virtuality operating it.

Because at least American 3D animation strives for the utmost in naturalism, there is no distance to fantasy content. Fantasy isn't special any more. It's down-to-earth and plain, like a daydream.

"CREATION"

Everything has to be "lifelike." That was the main goal right from the beginning, although, outwardly, it began with a doctoral thesis finished in 1963: *Sketchpad: A Man-Machine Graphical Communications System* by Ivan Sutherland.

> Sketchpad may look obvious and under-powered as a drawing program from today's perspective but nothing like it had existed before. Sutherland introduced many of the graphical conventions we now take for granted.
>
> It used a scale of 2000:1, making the virtual drawing space huge, and pioneered techniques such as "rubberbanding," zooming and object-oriented drawing. A light pen provided coordinates for drawing commands entered using the keyboard. Previously drawn primitive objects could be recalled and rotated, scaled and moved. Finished drawings could be stored on magnetic tape and re-edited at a later date.[4]

In 1963, the inventor was drafted into the army, and at the age of 26, First Lieutenant Ivan Sutherland was given control of $15 million dollars a year and told to "go sponsor computer research."

One of the early matchmakers between scientific research and Hollywood is still active today on a grand scale. Edwin E. Catmull is president of Pixar Animation Studios; back then, he was a member of the University of Utah's computer science department:

> While completing his doctorate, Catmull worked on some of first computer-generated experiments that made it into Hollywood film. He created an animated version of his own hand, for example, that was seen in the 1976 sci-fi thriller *Futureworld*.[5] *Thanks to that movie, the first actor to get a digital doppelganger in a feature film was Peter Fonda. They projected a raster onto Fonda's white-painted face, which was photographed from two angles. The result was used as reference for the computer model to get a rotating robot head that transforms from a simple polygon model into a plastic-like shining actor's head. The image was created by Triple-I in cooperation with computer graphics pioneer John Whitney, Jr.*

But the timing wasn't right: *The dreamsmiths were unprepared for the total forge.*[6]

The process to depict real people at that time for more than a few seconds as in *Futureworld* proved too difficult, and audiences wouldn't appreciate the crude lightcycle vector graphics of *Tron* or the 3D games aesthetic of *Last Starfighter*. They disliked the images as being cold and soulless.

A few years later, some dead film stars were resurrected thanks to Nadia Magnenat Thalmann's *Rendez-vous in Montreal* (1987) and the business acumen of their heirs. Marilyn Monroe and Humphrey Bogart, W. C. Fields and Marlene Dietrich were among the first to become "immortal" that way. But even the proprietors of the Berlin Film Museum that covered much of Marlene's career, costumes, and memorabilia rejected the Dietrich clone for their shrine. The Goddess didn't look like a goddess but like a piece of digital clay. The face was awkward, totally artificial, and bore no resemblance to the movie star.

So the virtual dreamsmiths took appropriate steps and turned to different breeds of characters that were easier to cast digitally. Even God didn't start his creation process with man. If there were to be human shapes at that time, the digital artists had to be content with robots (Robert Abel's 1985 *Sexy Robot* TV commercial, a simple forerunner of motion capture, with the live-action painstakingly displayed on TV monitors) or toys.

But as we know: good bait catches fine fish. And the right bait came with the introduction of the PC: the personal computer and all those commercials using the distortion technique of morphing.

Now there was suddenly one "quantum jump" after another. After Steven Spielberg and Dennis Muren's digitally created dinosaurs in the 1993 *Jurassic Park* (the first came to us as Winsor McCay's 2D *Gertie the Dinosaur*), after John Lasseter's *Toy Story* two years later, after *Ice Age* (2002) mammals and Scrat, the acorn-obsessed saber-toothed squirrel, after *Nemo* (2003) and other fish, the evolution of animation brought caricatures of human beings and eventually the hoped-for "lifelike" people. In their striving for photo-realism, Americans still seem to have problems reproducing believable human beings, but in the long run, synthetic actors are unavoidable, as we all need those ghostly avatars representing us in the world wide web of digital images. That is where live actors come in again.

BATMAN FOREVER

Biomechanics organizations monitored and tracked the human body's motions for medical research. Multiple cameras were synced to a computer to monitor and register the body's motions for medical research. Reflective or bright markers placed on the body's main points of motion (elbows, wrists, knees) could help track movements.

The video game industry was among the first to introduce this system to the entertainment industry, and John Dykstra used it for creating a digital double of Val Kilmer in *Batman Forever* (1995), produced by Tim Burton and directed by Joel Schumacher.

Jeff Kleiser was one who spearheaded the process. In 1986, while working at Omnibus Computer Graphics, he used an optical system from motion analysis to encode martial arts movement for a test for Marvel Comics, but back then the result was disappointing. When Omnibus closed down, Kleiser joined forces with Diana Walczak, an expert in sculpting human bodies. Together they founded Kleiser-Walczak Construction Company with the clear objective to build and animate *Synthespians*, including the digital stunt doubles for Sylvester Stallone, Rob Schneider, and others in *Judge Dredd* (1995). They also created Jet Li's evil double from a parallel universe in *The One* (2001). The content became more and more stupid while the technology that was meant to transport it exploded in sophistication. This is when motion capture came in.

There were digital extras on board James Cameron's *Titanic* (1997) and in Ridley Scott's *Gladiator* (2000) that today wouldn't draw audiences from the woodwork. Then they applied the technique to fantasy creatures: Ahmed Best, the actor digitized for Jar Jar Binks, acted on the set of the *Star Wars* prequels in front of a blue screen opposite the other performers. He wore a special suit with markers and a Jar Jar headpiece.

Sinbad: Beyond the Valley of the Mists, a not too successful and meanwhile completely forgotten coproduction between India and the United States, used the technology in 2000 for a completely 3D-animated picture. They had two sets: one for the mocap performers and one for the voiceovers. It was a little bit like the early days of sound film when they did different language versions with foreign actors behind the set to speak the lines.

DIGITAL EVOLUTION AND DISNEYFICATION

The Disneyfication (or Disneyization) of computer graphics began with Pixar (Ed Catmull and John Lasseter, who was forced out of his executive chair in 2018 due to "alleged sexual misconduct" that made some staff members feel "disrespected and uncomfortable") and, instead of the stop motion-animated toys of Arthur Melbourne-Cooper, with the computer-generated *Toy Story* of 1994.

The big breakthrough of CGI in terms of photo-realism came with director Peter Jackson, Andy Serkis (as Gollum), and the *Lord of the Rings* trilogy. Those fantasy creatures finally developed into apes and the apes into men, and the artificial men are going to absorb the viewer or the so-called user.

The process of digital evolution brought this technique from the background to the foreground, where it became standard not only in the world of make-believe but in daily life as well: monetary transactions, working environments, infrastructure, surveillance, warfare, and so on. All of a sudden, everybody would wear bits and pieces of this technology around, work with it, and "play" with it.

It all reminds me of a story written by Jack Finney in 1954: "The Body Snatchers." It was filmed four times. Back then, in Cold War McCarthyism, the pod people were meant to represent the "communist menace." But there is a deeper meaning.

You will find Finney's "pod people" everywhere in society: unspeakable "demons" who are going to take possession of friends, parents, relatives, neighbors. According to Finney, even lovers turn inexplicably cold, succumb to depression, or become victims of dementia—and we fear that we are next in line to lose our mind and soul!

REFERENCES

1. Tony White, *The Animator's Workbook*. Oxford: Phaidon Press Limited, 1986, p. 158.
2. Jim Danforth, *The Significance of Naturalistic Stop Motion Animation*. Reprinted with kind permission of the author.

3. Béla Balázs, *Early Film Theory*. New York/Oxford: Berghahn Books, 2010, p. 174.

4. Ivan Sutherland, Father of Graphics. June 16, 2016. https://www.i-programmer.info/history/people/329-ivan-sutherland.html

5. Edwin E. Catmull, Biography. https://www.notablebiographies.com/newsmakers2/2004-A-Di/Catmull-Edwin-E.html

6. Theodor Nelson, *Computer Lib/Dream Machines*, 2nd ed. Self-published, 1974. Redmond, Washington: Tempus Books of Microsoft Press, 1987.

CHAPTER 8

The Decomposition of Images

THE TECHNOLOGY OF THE age of virtualization mediates a little of that feeling of omnipotence that Stanley Kubrick described showing a star child at the end of *2001: A Space Odyssey*. In new media, we are no more viewers and consumers but participate actively.

SPEAKING LIONS AND CENTAURS

In the cyber age, the magic word to open sesame is no more analogue, no more cinema or TV, but crossmedia, IPTV (Internet Protocol Television), mobile phones, iPads, ADSL (Asymmetric Digital Subscriber Line) TV, and so on. Everything and everybody is subject to a global network. In the beginning, it was just a typewriter in front of a TV set. Today it is a life design that fulfills the visions of religion. Anything can be copied and look real digitally—be it reasonable or tasteless. Like an ancient God, more powerful than Harryhausen, you can cross life forms, animals, and humans and create your own *Chronicles of Narnia*: populated with talking lions, centaurs with ponytails, winged unicorns, and other exotic chimera. According to the viral marketing of a Swiss chocolate manufacturer, the future of cows is purple.

The mediator between the products of the human brain and global reality is the internet. The internet is, so to speak, a byproduct of the 1969 ARPANET, a project of the Advanced Research Project Agency (ARPA) installed by the United States Ministry of Defense.

Helmut Herbst, a German professor and filmmaker, developed a theory about what he called the decomposition of images that began with Robertson's *Phantasmagoriae,* his ghostly magic lantern projections in the nineteenth century, and reached its final stage with the internet. To put such images into a general store with drawers or transform it into a box office at the entrance of a cinema is like nailing a pudding to the wall.

The content of *Star Wars, Star Trek,* et al. is not science fiction but the technology that makes these images possible. George Lucas once postulated to "democratize" such means of production. The result is to be seen on YouTube, a rather young medium that already contains billions of moving images in its brief history. The population boom led to an explosion of (mostly amateur) images. Everybody seems to feel a vocation to participate in that cult. Mediocrity has become the main competition of the professionals.

CYBERPUNK

In William Gibson's *Neuromancer* vision of cyberpunk virtual reality, man virtually becomes part of the computer world:

> ...a "consensual hallucination" created by millions of connected computers. This network can be "jacked" into, while in the real world characters flit from Tokyo to the Sprawl, an urban agglomeration running down the east coast of the US. Gritty urban clinics carry out horrendous sounding plastic surgery. A junkie-hacker, Case, is coaxed into hacking the system of a major corporation. What once seemed impossibly futuristic is now eerily familiar.

Neuromancer, says novelist and blogger Cory Doctorow, remains a vividly imagined allegory for the world of the 1980s, when the first seeds of massive, globalised wealth-disparity were planted, and when the inchoate rumblings of technological rebellion were first felt. A generation later, we're living in a future that is both nothing like the Gibson future and instantly recognizable as its less stylish, less romantic cousin. Instead of *zaibatsus* [large conglomerates] run by faceless salarymen, we have doctrinaire thrusting young neocons and neoliberals who want to treat everything from schools to hospitals as businesses.[1]

Raymond Kurzweil, Google's chief futurist and director of engineering, claims that we are close to linking our brains with AI. This wouldn't make our brain obsolete, though: *By linking our brains to cloud computers, humans could expand the limits of our own computing ability—and eventually, upload our own brains to the cloud.*[2] Kurzweil hopes that in the 2030s or 2040s, our thinking will be predominately nonbiological and that we will be able to fully back up our brains.

Larry Page, Google's cofounder, hopes that the functions of the search engine will someday become part of the human brain. Google, of course, will be the supranational institution to select these implants.

Raúl Rojas, professor of artificial intelligence, Free University Berlin, considers the Silicon Valley visions of coming singularity illusory and phantasmal. *We are far apart from understanding the brain let alone surpass it.*[3] But this is not the question. These ideas are being *thought*, and this alone makes them real. Artificial vision, brain-computer interfaces (BCIs), and mind-machine interfaces (MMIs) are science fact. The attack on the human brain is well underway. *The Amazing Transparent Man* is not only a film by Edgar G. Ulmer but, beginning with Facebook, naked scanners, surveillance cameras, and flying-eye drones, a desirable concept for global totalitarianism. Destination: open the human subconscious mind.

Where does the Orwellian vision begin, and where does it end? How high will the level of immersion be?

My old-fashioned stop-motion nostalgia is only partly nostalgia. It's more concern about the social consequences of the global standardization of mind control. The power will belong not to the user, but whoever will control him or her.

Three-dimensional animation and digital games are only a piece of the jigsaw in a global concept. Europe, for instance, stands for variety but not for interactive randomness. We cannot suspend or delay a process, but we want to save our poetry, our music, our culture. It's a question of ethics.

Traditional animation is part of that culture.

REFERENCES

1. Ed Cumming, William Gibson: The Man Who Saw Tomorrow. *The Guardian*, July 28, 2014.
2. Solomon Israel, *Artificial intelligence, human brain to meet in the 2030s, says futurist Kurzweil.* June 9, 2015. Kurzweil Accelerating Intelligence. http://www.kurzweilai.net/
3. Stefan Mey, *Droht uns die Herrschaft der Roboter?* In: Spiegel Online, June 23, 2015. http://www.spiegel.de/netzwelt/gadgets/robokratie-rezension-des-buches-von-thomas-wagner-a-1040055.html

CHAPTER 9

Aardman, or
A Renaissance
of Stop Motion

WE SHOULD JUDGE SUCH wonderful Pixar productions as *Finding Nemo, Ratatouille,* or *Coco* not by their digital virtues but by story and character animation—and tantamount (!) to *Anomalisa,* written and codirected by Charlie Kaufman, a unique amalgam of animation processes that combine puppets with CG and the use of 3D-printed stop-motion animation, or the truly intercultural poetry of Laika's *Kubo and the Two Strings*:

> 4.3 seconds. That's how much of a scene a stop-motion animator completes on an average shooting week during a Laika movie production. Unless you're a speed reading champ, it probably took you that long to read this sentence. [...]
>
> Hundreds of people from all over the world, in dozens of departments, with skills honed in specific niches of any number of industries will generate hundreds of

thousands of things: scraps of fabric testing patterns, dyes, construction techniques; 2D character sketches; printouts of research materials; a custom motion control setup built around a bowling ball; a boy's face with one eye open and one closed, a boy's face with one eye open and the other open just a sliver, a boy's face with one eye open and the other open slightly more and one corner of the mouth beginning to rise into a crooked smile...[1]

Why should such art be old-fashioned and outdated?

SYMBIOSIS BETWEEN STOP MOTION AND COMPUTER-GENERATED IMAGERY

Maybe it would be if the powers of the cultural industries had to decide—but thanks to Peter Lord and David Sproxton, that didn't happen, and Lord and Sproxton were clever enough to create popular clay characters that worked great with audiences worldwide: Wallace and Gromit and Shaun the sheep.

In a 20-year old interview, Peter Lord spoke about the secret of hands-on animation:

...there is something about working with the materials. There is a fundamental difference between working with your hands and your arms and your fingertips, and working on the keyboard. I don't know.... For all of us animators at Aardman now, we are trained in this craft, just like a musician or a painter, it's all hand and head, hand and brain. One of the guys said to me just the other day: "When I animate," he said, "I can do it by sound." I think he was dreaming actually, but he said that when he animates a puppet, it's the sound of the joint moving that he's aware of. This type of experience indicates how instinctive and tactile our art is. You grab the puppet with two hands, and you feel the whole thing move, you feel the twist of the chest away from the hips, the roll of the shoulders.... The camera has to move right, the light has to be right, the actor has to do the right thing—make-up, costume, everything has to be right. Just for one moment in time. That's the way we work. I believe that the humanity in what we're doing, the process, all comes through in the final film.[2]

Of course, Aardman is using CGI devices, too. In a certain way, digital technology was instrumental in reviving and bringing back the process of stop motion:

Once frame grabbing software was brought into the mix and animators could instantly see their animation, the gloves came off and the new Renaissance of Stop Motion Animation had arrived. The very first frame grabber that I personally know of was created at Will Vinton Studios using a tape machine to capture on video cassette and a few frames of animation could be played back. The very first software framegrabber is a little bit of a debate but officially Adobe's Premier would allow you to framegrab from a camera and play back the animation. This is most likely the first commercial release of a software capable of doing this. Later software like Frame Thief and Monkey Jam would be released to hobbyists interested in animating at home. Next would come Stop Motion Pro which was used by Aardman for many years as their framegrabber, along with AnimatorDV which later became Animator HD. But the software that became the industry standard in the US would become DragonFrame. Originally called Dragon, DragonFrame would for the first time be an affordable software that was available on the Mac OS and Windows operating systems, along with offering highend features and stability only found in the more expensive counterparts. DragonFrame literally changed the game for everyone in the field of animation and made all its competitors stand up and take notice.[3]

Aardman's swashbuckler *The Pirates! In an Adventure with Scientists!*, released in 2012, blends traditional model animation with state-of-the-art CGI technology:

> The Pirate Captain has been sculpted over an armature—a steel skeleton of ball-and-socket joints. His hat is made from Fast Cast resin. His hair, moustache, coat and trousers are foam latex.
>
> His brow is modeling clay, his eyes resin, his belt buckle brass and his boots silicone. The most complex element to construct was his head, which was first sculpted, then scanned. "Scan data is used to build and sculpt a new head on the computer," [puppet designer Andrew] Bloxham says. "That head is then split into pieces separating the mouth-shape area." He produces a tray of perhaps 200 versions of the character's mouth, representing every conceivable shape. "The mouth is 'rigged' in CGI so that it can be moved, sculpted and animated into each of the hundreds of mouth shapes required. When this is completed, the mouths and head are printed out in rapid-prototyping machines, cured with UV light, then sanded and painted by hand." […]
>
> Pirates! is being on top-of-the-range Canon EOS ID digital still cameras—which were also used for the BBC *Wallace & Gromit* series—rather than Aardman's collection of "bunny-eared" Mitchell classic film cameras, which have been retired. "We've got 40 Mitchells, which cost us a fortune, in storage," Lord says. Digital still cameras speed up the process, as do CGI effects. […]
>
> CGI, meanwhile, has liberated Aardman in other ways, allowing it to stretch itself creatively. "Within our specialist world, I'm a whore! I'm shameless!" Lord says, dismissing the notion that he is a stop-frame animation purist. "I don't worry about theoretical purity. I just want

to hear the technician at my shoulder saying, 'I can do that'—and you know they will. What charms me is being able to take our handmade world and make it bigger; free it up a bit."[4]

AN INHERENT CHARM FOR HALF THE PRICE

To Henry Selick, another stop-motion legend, who graduated from CalArts and started as a traditional Disney animator in the 1970s, the process of stop motion and replacement animation combines all of his favorite things—sculpture, drawing, photography, music, and physics: *Stop-motion is sort of twitchy. If we were to remove that completely, there'd be no point in it. After all, the beauty and mystery of this craft are in those traces of the animator's hand.*[5]

There's an inherent charm as well as a certain reality (in stop-motion) that you can't get any other way. Real materials, real cloth, real puppets and there on the screen bathed in real light.[6]

Selick is known for his work on Tim Burton's *The Nightmare Before Christmas* (1993), *James and the Giant Peach* (1996), and *Coraline* (2009) with Laika. At a young age, he was influenced by both Lotte Reiniger and *The Adventures of Prince Achmed* and Ray Harryhausen and *The 7th Voyage of Sinbad*.

All of this is elaborate stop-motion, but you can have the fun for half the price, as the Belgian series *A Town Called Panic* (*Panique au village*) proves: the everyday adventures of the small figurines of three roommates, Cowboy, Indian, and, as the main character, Horse, in a rural village. There certainly is not much animation used to move these mostly stiff figures, but they have character and personality. The producers, Stéphane Aubier and Vincent Patar, play it out like children who have toy figures. Everything will end in a mess and anarchic madness, from village to inferno.

REFERENCES

1. Thomas Ross, *Poetry in Stop-Motion.* https://moviepilot.com
2. Wendy Jackson, An Interview With Aardman's Peter Lord. *Animation World Magazine* (22), May 1997.
3. *The History of Stop Motion—In A Nutshell.* June 4, 2016. http://www.stopmotionmagazine.net/history-stop-motion-nutshell
4. James Silver, *How Aardman Is Embracing the Digital Age.* November 2, 2010. https://www.wired.co.uk/article/aardman-morphs
5. Henry Selick, *Keeping Stop-Motion Moving Ahead*, by Neda Ulaby. February 5, 2009. https://www.npr.org/templates/story/story.php?storyId=100156290
6. Bill Jones, *He Kept His* Nightmare *Alive. The Phoenix Gazette.* October 22, 1993.

CHAPTER 10

The Isle of Old-Fashioned Animators

PANDORA'S BOX

We simply need that old *sense of wonder* to avoid becoming exclusively digital.

Dennis Muren, who turned away from photographing stop-motion type films in favor of CGI (and thereby, en passant, opened Pandora's Box), said:

> Almost anyone can do effects now, and so we have people out there happily turning out images, whether they have any talent or not. Effects are so commonplace that if I were growing up today, I don't know that the spark would be there to attract me. But lots of young people *are* attracted—some of whom consider us old-timers practically obsolete. We have people now at *ILM* who look at the work we did

on *Star Wars* like people of my generation used to look at silent movies.[1]

Developments happen fast, sometimes in a matter of seconds, on the verge of social virtualization. At the same time, we are losing a lot of our haptic expertise. More and more, critical voices are raised:

> Guy Standing, a British economist and author of *The Precariat*, argues that globalization "commodifies" everything, increasing the number of people doing insecure forms of work. The precariat [a social class formed of people suffering from precarity] works when and in whatever circumstances employers choose, creating short-term jobs that lead to a short-term lifestyle with little hope of building a future or a career.
>
> In the media and entertainment industry, we have seen the gradual commoditization of premium content (the music industry as a case in point), so a similar effect on work and jobs could also be expected. Standing believes that because of its constant distractions, online connectivity conditions people towards a general short-term philosophy on life.[2]

IT CAME FROM MEGASAKI

In February 2018, the Berlin International Film Festival (*Berlinale*) for the first time in its history opened with a stop-motion entry: *Isle of the Dogs*. For festival director Dieter Kosslick, this hadn't to do with a passion for animation but more with friendship with director Wes Anderson. After all, Anderson came from the world of "real" or "legitimate" movies (*The Grand Budapest Hotel*), and there was the chance of getting some big-name voice actors like Jeff Goldblum, Tilda Swinton, Scarlett Johansson, and Bill Murray to walk on Kosslick's sponsored red carpet. But it was understood as a signal, too. Many guests were surprised that a so-called "A" festival would open with a film like that. Why, of all people, would an acknowledged director of live-action films descend (!) to the world of stop motion?

It's well known that for Wes Anderson, the world is one big toy box. His new picture is set in a near-future Japan, where Kobayashi (voiced by Kunichi Nomura, one of the film's co-writers), the corrupt mayor of fictional city Megasaki, has taken draconian measures to curb the spread of various canine diseases, including the dreaded "snout fever." He orders all Megasaki's dogs to be exiled to a bleak island, essentially a huge offshore trashpile.

Dogs are treated like garbage. But then Atari comes, the 12-year old son of the dog-hating, cat-loving mayor, to save his beloved dog.

The puppet dogs' expressive eyes may occasionally well up with tears, but if there's one thing that *Isle of Dogs* isn't, it's twee; Anderson and his story collaborators, who also include Roman Coppola and Jason Schwartzman, firmly eschew the Japanese cult of *kawaii*, or cuteness.[3]

If you watch the stop-motion films produced by institutions like the *Laika* studio (*Coraline* and *The Corpse Bride*) or *Aardman Animations* (Wallace and Gromit), you'll see their work is all about the minutiae and manipulating even the smallest design elements.

And Anderson, no matter if he's working in stop-motion or live-action, is positively *obsessed* with minutiae. He loves all the tiny components of *mise en* scène that seem trifling in a vacuum. He's in utmost control of every bit of visual information that appears in each frame. And like an animator, he'll often use his total mastery over the frame to exaggerate effects, lending even his live-action films a cartoonish quality.[4]

The reviewer goes so far as to call the fable about dogs, pro-cat bureaucracy, and trash-strewn wastelands an *abundant homage to the great Japanese filmmaker Akira Kurosawa*.

This praise seems really outrageous for animation, but it's also a much-needed plea for the possibilities of dimensional animation. Indeed, the film is a mix of two Japanese filmmakers: Kurosawa and Hayao Miyazaki.

Isle of Dogs was two years in the making. A crew of 670 handled 1000 puppets: 500 dogs and 500 humans.

> We tried to do everything we can in the camera, *Anderson explained*, and I don't think there is anything in the whole movie that you would call CG.[5]

Anderson also explained that it's definitely not a children's movie. For some children, it could even be disturbing. And he points out the acceptance of animation in Japan within the adult community: *Miyazaki is Spielberg-level in popularity*.

But why would *he* do it?

Anderson has a lot of intellectual reasons to give, but suddenly he digs deep into his biography and unearths memories from his childhood.

One shouldn't forget that Anderson already started in stop motion by producing *The Fantastic Mr. Fox* from a book by Roald Dahl, a picture that felt like a return to the days of Starevich and *The Story of the Fox*.

> …it was the first Roald Dahl book that I ever read as a child, and I became a huge fan of Dahl, and he was a big part of my childhood. For some reason, this book was the one I always kept with me. […]
>
> And at a certain point I started thinking I would like to do a stop-motion film, and a stop-motion film with puppets with fur. And this really, you know, it was a good opportunity for that. This connected with that.

To bring it to life through some sort of handmade process, that's just like a sort of magic: *It's like toys.*

And then it comes:

> Yeah, I loved *King Kong*. You know, when I grew up, I think when I became aware of stop-motion was—I can't remember the name of the guy—Willis, maybe? Something like Willis [O'Brien] is the guy who did the stop-motion on *King Kong*, and his protégé was Ray Harryhausen, who's sort of the most famous stop-motion guy ever. And he did a number—and the ones that I saw were the ones that are sort of Greek mythology—*Seventh Voyage of Sinbad, Jason and the Argonauts*, there's another Sinbad movie also, things like *Clash of the Titans.*
>
> Those movies all have a big stop-motion element to them, and I really loved them as a kid. And also there were these TV—the holiday specials that the *Rankin-Bass Company* did, the *Rudolph the Red-Nosed Reindeer*, and there was one about—there's one that's sort of the story of how Santa Claus came to be. Those were ones that I—we were—my brothers and I were really taken with.[6]

Arthur Rankin, Jr., who produced those perennial animated Christmas specials with his partner Jules Bass, passed away in 2014. This is how he remembered it in an interview:

> A trade delegation had come to America from Japan. There was one gentleman who represented the steel industry... another who was in textiles. And a third who represented their motion picture industry. The motion picture representative had a studio he wanted to promote. He asked a friend of his in Washington D.C. if he could be introduced to one of America's foremost animators. And by mistake he was led to me (laughs). We got along very well. He had been born in the U.S.

and after he graduated college he went back to Japan. We became close friends. He invited me to come over, look at his studios, and tell him what I thought. I did. I went over, toured the studios and saw an example of stop motion, which hadn't been done in a long time and not in any great depth. I was very taken by it... I thought it was a new approach. Of course I got to re-design it but I used the technique. We started out making some short films and they turned out very well. I made a series that I syndicated about *Pinocchio*. And then *Rudolph the Red-Nosed Reindeer* lit up his nose.[7]

The real star of *Rudolph*, however, was an Asian animation director who was respected in Japan as well as in China.

FANG MING, A.K.A. MOCHINAGA-SAN

The Chinese in the north had a film studio in Changchun but didn't know much about animation back then. Their first animated films were done by Fang Ming. But Fang Ming was not Chinese. Actually, Fang Ming was the Chinese name [translated *Bright Direction*] of Japanese animator Mochinaga Tadahito (the man who later trained Kawamoto). Mochinaga's Puppet Animation Film Studio in Tokyo was associated with client Rankin/Bass's *Animagic* stop-motion specials, such as the perennial NBC Christmas favorite *Rudolph the Red-Nosed Reindeer* (1964) and the horror spoof *Mad Monster Party* (1967, cowritten by *Mad* editor Harvey Kurtzman), which featured the voice of Boris Karloff.

Born in Tokyo on April 1, 1919, Mochinaga moved to Manchuria with his family. His father worked at the South Manchuria Railway Company. Young Mochinaga spent his elementary school days in China and so became familiar with the Chinese culture. From time to time, family members took him to Tokyo. There he saw a Mickey Mouse cartoon when he was 10 years old. During his junior high school days in Tokyo, Mochinaga saw another Disney *Silly Symphony* in Technicolor, *Water Babies,* which captured him with its beauty. This experience inspired him to become an animator.

During his three years as an art school student in Tokyo, Mochinaga devoted his time to studying the techniques of animated filmmaking. His graduate work, in 1938, was a short film: *How to Make Animated Films*.

Mochinaga was the first Japanese to build a multiplane camera (four levels) and also participated in Japanese war propaganda. His first directorial assignment, *Fuku-chan's Submarine* (1944), showed an attack on an enemy cargo ship.

In 1945, accompanied by his faithful wife Ayako, he returned to Manchuria. In Changchun, he was asked to join the art department of Man-Ei (Manchuria Film Studio), with 2000 employees the largest film studio in Asia in those days. Under Japan's surrender on August 15, 1945, Man-Ei was disbanded and the company handed over to the Chinese. Fang Ming, however, would stay and instruct the Chinese filmmakers in 2D and 3D animation before he returned to Japan and associated with Arthur Rankin, Jr., and Jules Bass.

PARANORMAN AND THE BOXTROLLS

While we are talking about them, here's another lover of *Rudolph* and Ray Harryhausen. His name is Travis Knight, and he is the head of Laika Entertainment, the Portland, Oregon studio that gave us *Coraline, ParaNorman, The Boxtrolls*, and the amazing *Kubo and the Two Strings*:

> It's been quite a journey, much like the unlikely stories of our characters. When I was a kid, I adored it, specifically stop motion animation. I loved the Rankin Bass holiday specials, but above all I loved the Ray Harryhausen creature features. I think the thing that made me a little bit unusual is that I wanted to learn how to do it. Like so many animators of my generation went down into their parents' basements, completely self taught, as an artist, as an animator.

Knight eventually hit it professionally with Will Vinton Studios and Claymation:

> The best thing about working [for] TV and commercials is that you have to crank through a lot of footage quickly. I got a ton of professional experience in a short time.[8]

Travis Knight became "the man who brought stop-motion animation into the 21st century":

> Historically, for a stop-motion film, you gathered the crew together, you made the movie, and then everyone ran screaming to the next project. But we have a core team. By going from film to film together like we have, all the innovations that happen over the course of making a film, from 3-D printing our characters' faces in color to advances in rigging or lighting, stay with us. All of the things we learned on *Coraline* we applied to *ParaNorman*, and all of the things we learned on *ParaNorman* and *Coraline* we applied to *The Boxtrolls*. In the time that we've been making films, every single department has achieved dramatic technical innovations. And those gains enable us to be more expansive in the kind of films we make. [...]
>
> Historically, there's been a degree of sameness to animated films. But we see animation as more than a genre. It's a powerful visual medium that can be used to tell virtually every kind of story in virtually any kind of genre. [...]
>
> The atmosphere here crackles with energy; people are constantly coming up with new ideas. I think that in large measure that's because of the fusion of different disciplines that we have—Luddites, craftspeople who don't know a thing about technology, converging and working with futurists, people who do nothing but try to figure

out the next thing, the next bit of cutting-edge technology they can bring to the process. They don't always play well together, but often the best solutions come out of that tension.[9]

To Travis Knight—as to Ray Harryhausen as to Peter Lord, back to Trnka, Zeman, and Starevich—*stop motion is a combination of imagination, physical exertion, and mental math capability*:

> One second of stop-motion animation film is made up of 24 unique, individual poses for each frame (24 frames per second). Multiply this by 60 seconds, and that means for every minute, there are 1440 unique, individual poses. Then multiply this by 90 minutes, the average length of a feature film, and you've got almost 130,000 unique, individual poses that the stop-motion animator has to create. According to Knight, it's all worth it. At the end of the process, each of those 130,000 poses adds up to something magical: inanimate objects coming to life to tell a story that delivers an emotional impact on the audience.[10]

Stop-motion work in progress: *Three Tuvans*.

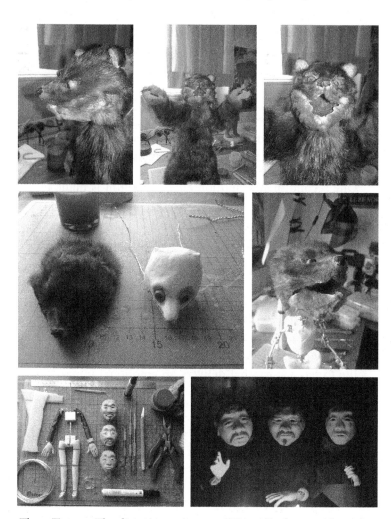

Three Tuvans. The directing animator, Grigori Zurkan, graduated from Film University Babelsberg. (Courtesy of Grigori Zurkan.)

REFERENCES

1. Don Shay, *Dennis Muren—Playing It Unsafe!* In: Cinefex, Number 65, March 1996.
2. Claudio Cocorocchia, *How the Digitization of Work Affects Us All.* January 19, 2016. http://www.weforum.org. The article refers

to Guy Standing's book *The Precariat: The New Dangerous Class.* London: Bloomsbury Academic, 2001.

3. *Isle of Dogs* Review—Wes Anderson's Scintillating Stop-Motion Has Bite. *The Guardian*, February 15, 2018.

4. Andy Crump, *How Wes Anderson Sneaks Stop-Motion Animation into Every Film He Makes.* March 28, 2018. http://www.theweek.com

5. Wes Anderson on the Politics of "Isle of Dogs" and a Return to Stop-Motion. *Variety*, February 15, 2018.

6. *For Wes Anderson, A "Fantastic Animated Adventure."* Radio Interview by Terry Gross. http://www.npr.com. March 26, 2010.

7. *Rankin/Bass' Arthur Rankin Jr. Chats about His Timeless Christmas Specials.* December 25, 2013. https://mediamikes.com

8. Brendon Connelly, *Kubo And The Two Strings* director, and Laika founder, Travis Knight, talks to us through making a stop motion movie. In: Den of Geek! January 18, 2017. http://www.denofgeek.com/us

9. Daitlin Roper, *The Man Who Brought Stop-Motion Animation to the 21st Century.* http://www.wired.com. September 18, 2014.

10. Eric Baker, *Laika CEO's 3 Essential Insights on Stop-Motion.* August 18, 2016. https://nofilmschool.com

The Stop-Motion Chronicles

1898

James Stuart Blackton is said to have created *The Humpty Dumpty Circus*. The Guinness Book of Movie Facts and Feats credits this as "the first animated film using the stop-motion technique to give the illusion of movement to inanimate objects". I personally doubt the year of release as well as the assumed quality of animation. It's all based on speculation because it's a lost film. www.guinnessworldrecords.com/world-records/first-animated-film.

1899

Charlotte (Lotte) Reiniger born on June 2 in Berlin Charlottenburg.

1900

Aleksandr Lukich Ptushko born on April 10 in Lugansk.

Hermina Týrlová born on December 11 in Březové Hory.

1901

Ferdinand Diehl born on May 20 in Unterwössen, Bavaria.

1904

Louis (Lou) Bunin born on March 28 in Russia.

1907
Edwin S. Porter brings seven animated toy *Teddy Bears* onto the screen. The little picture is released by the Edison Manufacturing Company.

1908
The Humpty Dumpty Circus by James Stuart Blackton and Albert Smith.
Arthur Melbourne Cooper animates *A Dream of Toyland*.

György Pál Marczincsak (George Pal) born on February 1 in Cegléd, Austria-Hungary.

1909–10
First German stop-motion matches created by cinematographer Guido Seeber.

1910
Ladislas Starevich creates his first puppet film with jointed insects: *Lucanus Cervus*.

Cartoonist Émile Cohl animates *Le Tout Petit Faust* as puppet play.

Karel Zeman born on November 3 in Ostroměř, Austria-Hungary.

1912
Jiří Trnka born on February 24 in Pilsen-Petrohrad, Austria-Hungary.

1914–15
Willis Harold O'Brien enters the world of stop-motion with *The Dinosaur and the Missing Link: A Prehistoric Tragedy*.

1920
Raymond Frederick (Ray) Harryhausen born on June 29 in Los Angeles.

1925
The Lost World, based on Arthur Conan Doyle's novel, combines Willis O'Brien's stop-motion dinosaurs with live action.

1926

Lotte Reiniger's silhouette film *The Adventures of Prince Achmed* premieres in Berlin and Paris.

1932

George Pal produces his first dimensional animation featuring Oberst cigarettes in Berlin.

1933

The original *King Kong* was the *Star Wars* of its day:

> He was a king and a god in the world he knew, but now he comes to civilization merely a captive—a show to gratify your curiosity. Ladies and gentlemen, look at Kong, the Eighth Wonder of the World.

Although you see the fingerprints of animators Willis O'Brien and assistant Buzz Gibson on the rabbit fur that model maker Marcel Delgado was given for the two Kong models, it's still the most memorable screen monster. The 18″ armatures of the puppets are not exactly the same: one Kong that was built earlier had a long face and looked a little bit human. The other one, with a rotund face, looked more like a gorilla.

1934

Oskar Fischinger follows George Pal's example with animated cigarettes that dance through an advertising film in Gasparcolor: *Muratti greift ein.*

Jan Švankmajer born on September 4 in Prague.

1936

Alexandr Lukich Ptushko's Soviet *The New Gulliver* (*Novyy Gullivyer*) has a live actor (Vladimir Konstantinovich Konstantinov, who died in 1944 in World War 2) go to the Kingdom of Lilliput and meet 1000 animated puppets.

1937

Starevich's feature-length *The Story of the Fox* (*Le roman de Renard*), based on the eleventh-century tale of *Reynard the Fox*, which was started in 1929 and finished by 1931, is finally released with a musical soundtrack added by Ufa in Germany.

The Seven Ravens (*Die sieben Raben*), a feature-length stop-motion film based on a fairy tale by the Brothers Grimm, with puppets created by Hermann Diehl and animated by his brother Ferdinand Diehl.

The Tale of the Fisherman and the Fish (*Skazka o rybake I rybke*), a color short film by Aleksandr Lukich Ptushko.

1940

James (Jim) Danforth born on July 13 in Ohio.

1943

In Zlín, Hermina Týrlová animates the adventures of *Ferda the Ant* (*Ferda Mravenec*).

1944

George Pal's *Puppetoons* awarded an Oscar.

1946

Revolt of the Toys (*Vzpoura hraček*) by Hermina Týrlová.

Charles R. Bowers, cartoonist, stop-motion animator and slapstick comedian, dies after a long illness on November 26 in Paterson, New Jersey.

1947

Jiří Trnka finishes his first feature-length puppet film, *The Czech Year* (*Špaliček*).

The Crab with the Golden Claws, a puppet-animated *Tintin* adventure from Belgium.

Stephen and Timothy Quay, twin brothers, born on June 17 in Norristown, Pennsylvania.

1949

Trnka gets international recognition with a puppet film version of Hans Christian Andersen's *The Emperor's Nightingale (Cisařův slavík)*.

Lou Bunin finishes his version of Lewis Carroll's *Alice in Wonderland*.

1950

Willis O'Brien honored with an Academy Award for animation and visual effects of another gorilla: *Mighty Joe Young*. "OBie" was assisted by Ray Harryhausen.

Jiří Trnka's *Prince Bayaya (Bajaja)*.

In Germany, Jugendfilm, a Berlin-based distribution company, releases a new feature-length project by the Diehl Brothers: *Always Lucky (Immer wieder Glück)*, introducing their version of Kasperl (Punch) Larifari.

1952

Neighbours: Pixilation made by Norman McLaren for National Film Board of Canada. Academy Award, Best Animated Short Film, 1953.

The Treasure of Bird Island (Poklad ptačího ostrava) by Karel Zeman.

Henry Selick born on November 30 in Glen Ridge, New Jersey.

1953

Ray Harryhausen animates a dinosaur awakened by radioactive tests at the North Pole: *The Beast from 20,000 Fathoms*.

Old Czech Legends (Staré pověsti české) by Jiří Trnka.

Peter Lord born on November 4 in Bristol, England.

1954

Michael Myerberg's *Hansel and Gretel* in Technicolor is released by RKO.

Karel Zeman has a group of boys travel back in time and encounter dinosaurs: *Journey to the Beginning of Time* (*Cesta do pravěku*).

1955

Trnka bases his version of the *Good Soldier Svejk* (*Dobrý voják Švejk*) on Josef Lada's original illustrations to Jaroslav Hašek's novel.

1958

The 7th Voyage of Sinbad has Ray Harryhausen creatures pursue Sinbad's men on the Island of Colossa: a Cyclops, a fire-breathing dragon, the double-headed giant bird Roc, and a sword-wielding skeleton.

1959

A Midsummer Night's Dream (*Sen noci svatojánské*), an ambitious puppet film version of Shakespeare's play directed by Jiří Trnka.

1961

Arthur Melbourne-Cooper dies on November 28 in Barnet, London.

1962

Willis O'Brien passes away on November 8 in Los Angeles.

1963

Jason and the Argonauts has seven sword-wielding skeletons from the magic hands of Ray Harryhausen.

George Pal's *The Wonderful World of the Brothers Grimm* features two three-strip Cinerama stop-motion sequences handled by Project Unlimited, a Hollywood outfit that was founded by Pal alumni Gene Warren and Wah Chang (with Tim Barr as third partner): elves animated by Don Sahlin and David Pal, George's son, and a jeweled dragon animated by Jim Danforth.

1964
Rudolph the Red-Nosed Reindeer with stop motion photographed in Japan by Tadahito Mochinaga and released by Rankin/Bass as Christmas TV special.

1965
The *Pillsbury Doughboy* is introduced in stop motion (animation by Cascade alumni Jim Danforth, David Allen, and others).

The Hand (*Ruka*), Trnka's final short film.

Ladislas Starevich dies on February 26 in Fontenay-sous-Bois.

1969
Jiří Trnka dies on December 30 in Prague.

1972
Aardman Animations is founded as low-budget shop by Peter Lord and David Sproxton.

1973
Alkesandr Ptushko dies on March 6 in Moscow.

Travis Andrew Knight, future CEO of Laika Entertainment, born on September 13 in Hillsboro, Oregon, a suburb of Portland.

1980
George Lucas' award-winning *The Empire Strikes Back* features a stop-motion sequence of Imperial Snow Walkers attacking the Rebel Alliance. The sequence was animated by Phil Tippett, Jon Berg, and Doug Beswick and photographed by Dennis Muren.

George Pal dies on May 2 in Beverly Hills.

1981
Lotte Reiniger dies on June 19 in Dettenhausen.

1982
The Flying Windmill (*Die fliegende Windmühle*), stop motion from East Germany's DEFA Studio für Trickfilme in Dresden, written and directed by Günter Rätz.

1983
Brian Cosgrove and Mark Hall transform Kenneth Grahame's children's novel *The Wind in the Willows* into a stop-motion feature.

1985
The Adventures of Mark Twain in Claymation from Will Vinton Studios.

1986
Street of Crocodiles by the Quay Brothers nominated at the Cannes Film Festival for a Golden Palm.

1988
Jan Švankmajer's version of Lewis Carroll's *Alice* (*Něco z Alenky*) is his first feature-length film.

1989
The man-and-dog pair *Wallace and Gromit* appears for the first time in Aardman's *A Grand Day Out*.

Karel Zeman dies on April 5 in Zlín, just a few months before the Velvet Revolution.

1990
German stop-motion short film *Balance* by brothers Christoph and Wolfgang Lauenstein wins Academy Award for Best Animated Short Film.

1991

Aardman wins Academy Award for *Creature Comforts.*

1992

With Spielberg, George Lucas, John Landis, Rick Baker, Dennis Muren, and others pushing for him, Ray Harryhausen is given an honorary Oscar (Gordon E. Swayer Award) for his lifetime achievement. Laudator is Tom Hanks.

Ferdinand Diehl dies on August 27 in his home in Gräfelfing near Munich next to his old puppet film studio.

1993

Stop-motion dinosaurs are changed to CGI by Dennis Muren for Steven Spielberg's *Jurassic Park.*

Hermína Týrlová dies on May 3 in Zlín.

1994

Lou Bunin dies on February 17 at the Actor's Fund Nursing Home in Englewood, New Jersey.

1996

Henry Selick turns Roald Dahl's book *James and the Giant Peach* into a feature-length puppet film.

1997

Tim Burton's *The Nightmare Before Christmas* involved the creation of 227 puppets with replacement heads. Henry Selick directed.

1999

Japanese animation expert Mochinaga Tadahito dies on April 1.

2000

Chicken Run, first feature-length animation by Aardman.

The British-Russian-American *The Miracle Maker*, a tale of the Christ, is recommended by Ray Harryhausen for the sheer number of puppets involved.

2002
A Town Called Panic (*Panique au village*), a very imaginative Belgian TV series by Vincent Patar and Stéphane Aubier.

2005
In *Corpse Bride*, Henry Selick again joins forces with director Tim Burton.

Aardman's feature-length *Wallace & Gromit: The Curse of the Were-Rabbit*.

2007
Shaun the Sheep created by Aardman.

The National Film Board of Canada short film *Madame Tutli-Putli* by Chris Lavis and Maciek Szczerbowski premieres in May at the film festival in Cannes.

2009
An exceptional year for the art of stop motion:

Mary and Max, an Australian entry, in January at the Sundance Film Festival.

Wes Anderson's adaptation of Roald Dahl's children's novel *Fantastic Mr. Fox* features the voices of George Clooney and Meryl Streep, but the real stars are animated puppets.

Laika Entertainment introduces *Coraline*, a girl's nightmare directed by Henry Selick.

2010
Acclaimed Japanese puppet designer and filmmaker Kawamoto Kihachirō dies on August 23.

2012

Laika Entertainment's *ParaNorman:* 11-year-old Norman is not only thrilled by horror movies, he can actually see ghosts. *ParaNorman* was animated by a crew of 300.

Aardman presents *The Pirates!*

2013

Ray Harryhausen dies on May 7 in his Kensington home in London.

2014

Laika's *The Boxtrolls*.

2015

Charlie Kaufman (screenwriter, *Being John Malkovich*) and animation director Duke Johnson join forces to create one of the most unusual stop-motion films. Puppets become people as they never were in *Anomalisa*.

2016

Kubo and the Two Strings (Laika Entertainment) is a staggering stop-motion story about a Japanese magic boy who fights the spirit of his evil grandfather, the Moon King. The American production captures the spirit of Japanese culture.

2018

Wes Anderson's *Isle of Dogs* opens the Berlin International Film Festival.

Aardman's prehistoric *Early Man*, a prehistoric sports comedy directed by Nick Park.

Bibliography

Albert Menache, *Understanding Motion Capture for Computer Animation and Video Games.* San Diego/San Francisco/New York/Boston/London/Sydney/Tokyo: Morgan Kaufmann/Academic Press, 2000.

Barry J. Purvis, *Stop-Motion Animation: Frame by Frame Film-Making with Puppets and Models.* Bloomsbury Publishing, 2014.

Béla Balázs, *Early Film Theory. Visible Man and the Spirit of Film.* Edited by Erica Carter, translated by Rodney Livingstone. New York/Oxford, 2010.

Giannalberto Bendazzi, *Cartoons: One Hundred Years of Cinema Animation.* Bloomington, IN: University of Indiana Press, 1994.

Giannalberto Bendazzi, *Animation: A World History.* Volumes I–III. Boca Raton, FL: CRC Press, Taylor & Francis Group. A Focal Press Book, 2015.

Isaac Kerlow, *The Art of 3D Computer Animation and Effects.* 4th ed. Hoboken, New York: Wiley, 2009.

Jaroslav Boček, *Jiří Trnka, Artist and Puppet Master.* 1st Eng. ed. Prague: Artia, 1965.

Jim Danforth, *Dinosaurs, Dragons & Drama: The Odyssey of a Trickfilmmaker.* Vol. 1 and Vol. 2. CD Books. Los Angeles: Archive Editions, 2012/2015.

Ken A. Priebe, *The Advanced Art of Stop-Motion Animation.* Boston: Cengage Learning PTR, 2010.

Klaus Kohlmann, *Der computeranimierte Spielfilm: Forschungen zur Inszenierung und Klassifizierung des 3-D-Computer-Trickfilms.* Bielefeld: transcript Verlag, 2007.

L. Bruce Holman, *Puppet Animation: History & Technique.* South Brunswick and New York: A. S. Barnes and Company. London: The Tantivy Press, 1975.

Leslie Cabarga, *The Fleischer Story.* Rev. ed. New York: DaCapo Press, 1988.

Lotte Reiniger, *Shadow Theatres and Shadow Films*. London and New York: B. T. Batsford and Watson-Guptill Publications, 1970.

Mike Hankin, *Ray Harryhausen: Master of the Majicks. Volume 1: Beginnings and Endings. Volume 2: The American Films. Volume 3: The British Films*. Los Angeles: Archive Editions, 2008–2013.

Orville Goldner and George E. Turner, *The Making of King Kong: The Story Behind a Film Classic*. New York: Ballantine Books, 1975.

Richard Fleischer, *Just Tell Me When to Cry: A Memoir*. New York: Carroll & Graf Publishers, Inc., 1993.

Richard Fleischer, *Out of the Inkwell: Max Fleischer and the Animation Revolution*. Lexington, KY: The University of Kentucky, 2005.

Rolf Giesen and Anna Khan, *Acting and Character Animation: The Art of Animated Films, Acting and Visualizing*. Boca Raton, FL: CRC Press, Taylor & Francis Group, 2017.

Rolf Giesen and J. P. Storm, *Animation under the Swastika: A History of German Trickfilm, 1933–1945*. Jefferson, NC: McFarland, 2012.

S.S. Wilson, *Puppets & People: Large-Scale Animation in the Cinema*. San Diego, CA: A.S. Barnes and Co. Inc., 1980.

Susannah Shaw, *Stop Motion: Craft Skills for Model Animation*. Oxford: Butterworth Heinemann, 2008.

The Art of Aardman. London: Simon & Schuster Ltd., 2016.

Tjitte De Vries and Ati Mul, *They Thought It Was a Marvel: Arthur Melbourne-Cooper (1874–1961: Pioneer of Puppet Animation)*. Amsterdam: Pallas Publications, 2010.

Tony White, *The Animator's Workbook*. Oxford: Phaidon Press Limited, 1986.

Valliere T. Richard, *Norman McLaren: Manipulator of Movement. The National Film Board Years, 1947–1967*. An Ontario Film Institute Book. London and Toronto: Associated University Press, 1982.

Index